# OVERCOMING PERFECTIONISM, ANXIETY, AND INDECISION

## A BRILLIANT BUT IMPERFECT GUIDE TO RELEASING YOUR INNER ACHIEVER

### CROSS BORDER BOOKS

# CONTENTS

# INTRODUCTION

*I am learning that perfection isn't what matters. In fact, it's the very thing that can destroy you if you let it.*

— EMILY GRIFFIN

Ah, perfectionism!

What a double-edged sword striving for perfection can be.

On the one hand, it can serve as a motivator, pushing you to perform at your best, achieving the best quality of work you could produce. On the other hand, perfectionism can lead to deep feelings of anxiety, procrastination, and a loss of time.

Can perfectionism be harnessed for all its positive attributes?

Can we mitigate the negatives?

How do we even measure our perfectionistic practices against our actual performance when we have been caught in the endless web of being perfect for so incredibly long?

Here's the reality about perfectionism—it is almost always rooted in deep fear and insecurity, and while we absolutely believe that it makes us better at what we do, there are few things that can create indecision as perfectionism can.

Most of us know that clinging to perfectionism is counter-productive yet somehow when we take on a new task, the same inefficient behaviors creep in.

If any of this sounds like you, don't despair!

Reigning in your perfectionistic proclivities is not as difficult as it sounds, and by channeling your strengths rather than succumbing to your fears, you can begin to take some of the pressure that you put on yourself off.

I know that all of this sounds like it is easier said than done, but the fact remains that if you truly want to be the highest achiever, some imperfection needs to be present in your work.

The reason for this goes beyond the perfectionist's inability to complete tasks—or to complete tasks but at a high cost to their mental health.

You see, true greatness is only achieved through the lessons we learn when we make imperfect mistakes—by their very nature, these are imperfect.

Some of the greatest minds the world has ever seen have had to overcome perfectionism, and ironically, it was the mistakes that propelled them into success and the history books.

Disgraced cyclist Lance Armstrong; historical painter and sculptor Michelangelo; and famed actress Emma Watson: All have overcome their struggles with perfectionism, learning to embrace the beauty and the opportunity to learn from their mistakes.

Perfection certainly isn't easy—but I don't have to tell you that, and perfection requires effort and time that most of us don't have.

Before I continue with what you will gain from reading this book, allow me to indulge you in my own story.

Years ago, I reached a turning point at the height of my perfectionism.

Upon reflection, it probably wasn't a turning point as much as it was an iron-clad door that slammed shut, preventing me from moving forward. Burnout nipped persistently at my heels as a reward for listening to the nagging critical inner voice that demanded flawlessness from me.

A once creative person, perfectionism had done so much more than robbed me of my creativity and productivity—my mental and physical health all seemed to have been up and gone once perfectionism came knocking.

While I knew without a shadow of a doubt that it was my job to regulate that inner voice, I just couldn't seem to shut it up, and ultimately, I bought into the idea that perfectionism was a good thing.

That is until one day, staring at the giant blank canvas of our outside wall, I realized—*"how many years had I been saying I was going to paint it? How many months have I agonized over perfectly filled cracks or the perfect color for an external boundary wall?"*

As I stood staring at the wall, I wondered how much of the rest of my life I had missed out on trying to metaphorically decide on how to perfectly fill the cracks and paint the walls of my life.

Steve Jobs was famed for taking eight years to pick a sofa, and I had laughed at the lunacy of that sentiment back then, yet here I was with a wall that was well overdue for a lick of paint, in burnout, and at breaking point, and still, I couldn't silence my inner critic.

"That was just a sofa... This is an entire wall! What will the neighbors think if I do a shoddy job?!"

I had taken a step back to examine my years-long preparation work, the open can of paint, and all the tools I had bought over the years to make my job easier when I decided to throw caution to the wind.

Stepping forward, I dipped the paintbrush into the paint and slapped an uncharacteristically wild and flawed stroke across the wall.

I stepped back to examine my mess and began laughing!

I shudder to think what the neighbors must have thought of my display, but that single stroke of paint began my journey of untangling myself from perfectionism.

Of course, it didn't free me immediately, and it took time, dedication, and a lot of time-outs for my inner critic to finally acquiesce and give up on being perfect, but I did free myself.

Striving for perfection is paralyzing, and often it just takes one wild stroke of a brush, or one tiny step forward to break this paralysis.

Did I make mistakes while painting that wall?

Sure, I did, but I realized that, as a perfectionist, aiming for adequate was simply not an option. So I learned to reflect inward and realize that the time and opportunities lost cost me financially, emotionally, and mentally far more than painting over the strokes that weren't perfect.

Let me ask you these two questions:

1. Are you using your time wisely?
2. Are you truly being productive?

If you're honest in answering these questions, you will find that both these answers are likely to be no, and in the same way, I was agonizing over a wall and just about everything else in my life, so are you.

I know it is difficult to contemplate right now and perhaps even overwhelming, but most of the time, getting things done less than perfectly is far more important than perfection.

Often, getting it done has far greater value than getting it done perfectly, and sweating the small stuff ultimately only leads you to feel a little overwhelmed. Perhaps even resentful that you cannot enjoy the little things in life.

But you probably know all of this, and you have chosen to purchase *Overcoming Perfectionism, Anxiety, and Indecision* because you are tired of living your life of indecision and perfection.

As a former perfectionist, I was not blind to the irony that a guide could be so magnificently imperfect—if I were aiming for perfection, this book would never have been read by you.

But brilliantly imperfect also implies you have a choice in whether you will succeed in breaking the bonds of perfectionism and, indeed, take back control of your life.

The burning question... Are you willing to take action and follow the steps in this book? Are you prepared to take action, even if that action is imperfect? In fact, I would encourage you to screw up in one way or the other when doing these exercises, just so that you can learn that failure is by no means fatal.

But first, you must undertake the journey of understanding why you are striving for the impossible in the first place. You need to dip your paintbrush directly into the tin and make your mark across the blank canvas that is the rest of your life, and find that it is possible.

Through the proven steps and techniques outlined in this book, and with guidance and understanding, you too can silence the voice that is perfectionism: Breaking free from the chains that are binding you, and painting a life that is rich with color and joy.

1

# THE OBSTACLES OF SUCCESS

At some point in our lives, we have all been affected by the drive to be perfect. In fact, according to a study by Momentum Leader, 92% of people will feel deeply affected by perfectionism during their lifetime (Intern, 2022).

This study, which was done with the University of Northern Colorado, gives a deep look at how trying to be perfect at work and in school can get in the way of success.

With 86% of people saying that perfectionism hurt their ability to get work done and 68% saying that perfectionism led to burnout, it's hard not to wonder why we strive for perfection so often.

## WHAT IS PERFECTIONISM?

We all knew that kid in school who seemed to have an endless list of achievements and accomplishments.

Perhaps you were that kid?

Perfection is an abstract concept, of course; in reality, it is nearly impossible. The issue with perfectionism is that it drives us to strive for the pot of gold at the end of the rainbow, and as we know, the gold doesn't exist, and the rainbow never stops moving.

One of the many bad things that happens when we try to be perfect is that we get so caught up in the idea that we lose sight of all the beautiful things life still has to offer.

I'm not saying some perfectionism isn't destructive—it's the equivalent of eating a couple of blocks of chocolate versus the entire slab—just enough, and you feel happy, but overdoing it, and the consequences are not pleasant.

Ultimately, perfection leads to procrastination, avoidance of challenges, and a mindset that believes that "all-or-nothing."

When we examine the statements and studies above and take a look at the dictionary definition of perfectionism—"a personal standard, attitude, or philosophy that demands perfection and rejects anything less" (*Definition of Perfectionism | Dictionary.com*, n.d.), it becomes a little easier to see why being perfect isn't humanly possible.

Perfectionism is toxic. It permeates every facet of our lives and every corner of society, from school to work, the way we relate to others and ourselves, and the creative activities we participate in, which should bring us relief from the stresses and strains of life.

### The Many Realms of Perfectionism

Being a perfectionist often starts in one area of our lives, moving swiftly to other areas until it consumes us.

This is because perfectionism, like so many other toxic things available to us, gives us a rush and a feeling of well-being until we fail to achieve perfect results again.

For many of us, the realm in which early perfectionism lingers starts at school, and some of us are great at being perfect in this setting.

Unfortunately, as we leave school and enter into university, college, or the workplace, perfectionism begins to bleed into other areas of our lives because perfection is just plain difficult outside of a safe scholarly and parental setting.

All of a sudden, we set impossible expectations not just for ourselves and our performance at work, but also for our loved ones, our kids (if we have any), our friends, and pretty much everyone else.

For some of us, our health suffers under the persistent pressure we place on ourselves, and our relationships fall apart.

Hygiene, our environment, how we speak and write, and even our physical appearance will eventually become consumed by wasted hours trying to be perfect

The perfectionist's life is lonely, filled with anxiety, and an endless need to chase that initial rush they got from the first time they did something perfect.

## THE RISE OF PERFECTIONISM

Perfectionism is nothing new, but lately, the need to be perfect is rising. Perfectionism is one of the most important reasons why depression and anxiety are on the rise among young adults, which is a very scary trend.

A study that looked at how perfectionism affects young adults found that social media is a big part of the problem. However, it would be unfair to say that social media is "the root of all evil," so we need to look at everything that is contributing to the perfection epidemic.

Now more than ever, people are pressured into earning more money, providing and receiving the best education, and self-driving pretty lofty career goals.

The measurement of status has shifted from social obligation and servitude to meritocracy, in which universities and workplaces encourage perfectionism through competition so that they can climb the economic and social ladder.

Meritocracy is the new social ideal. Everyone, from parents to politicians, emphasizes how to level the playing field through perfectionism so that meritocracy can reign supreme.

Like perfectionism, meritocracy is not imperfect as it negates the genetic lottery of being born aristocratic or wealthy. While I agree that wealth, advantage, and merit should be freely available to anyone who strives for it, it shouldn't come with the penalty of being perfect (Primack et al., 2017).

Human beings and nature are imperfect by default. We are not machines, and even then, if you've ever stared frustratedly at a frozen laptop, you will know that devices are flawed too.

Added to all this, globalization has increased competition within universities and organizations. More companies adopt a results-focused approach to performance, so employees feel the drive to outperform their colleagues.

Leaders and managers are under enormous pressure to push their employees to achieve exceedingly high goals, which takes a toll on the individuals who make up teams.

Strangely, people who burn out because of the pressure to be perfect make it harder for companies to find and keep good employees. This is because unhappy, stressed-out employees don't want to be a part of a society that expects them to be perfect.

### The Root Cause of Perfectionism

I want to clarify that science is still undecided on what causes people to strive toward perfectionism.

It is agreed that it is probably a combination of factors, including being diagnosed or living with an undiagnosed personality disorder like obsessive-compulsive personality disorder (OCPD), environment, and upbringing.

Added to this, when we have a history of being high achievers, we can sometimes feel a huge amount of pressure to live up to our past achievements.

Those with a history of achieving well are far more likely to engage in perfectionistic behaviors. This is especially true for adults who were overachievers as children.

A few of these perfectionist driving forces include:

- A fear of being disapproved of as well as a feeling of insecurity or inadequacy.
- A history of obsessive-compulsive disorder (OCD) or OCD tendencies—not to be confused with OCPD, which is a personality disorder.
- Having a parent who is a perfectionist or a parent who expresses disapproval if their child underperforms to their standards.
- Having a parent who places more emphasis on a child's results rather than their process.

- Having had an insecure or detached relationship with a primary caregiver or parent.

This list is by no means extensive, and just about anything could be a catalyst to a life of striving for perfection.

Regardless of the cause, perfectionism has a profound impact not just on our work but on our well-being.

### The Consequences of Perfectionism

Doing the same thing over and over, avoiding doing anything at all, or staying up all night to complete a task perfectly has some serious consequences.

The occasional all-nighter or putting the final touches on something from time to time isn't damaging, but when perfectionism begins to creep into every task and every facet of our lives, it causes more harm than good.

For example, a study found that students who are perfectionists are more likely to excel at school but are also far more likely to suffer from social anxiety and attempts at self-harm (Primack et al., 2017).

Not taking care of our well-being and mental health harms our physical health too, and high blood pressure, eating disorders, and the general health of our hearts all suffer.

Perfectionism, when left unchecked can cause you to

- enter into a deep depression.
- suffer from anxiety.
- increase your risk of eating disorders.
- cause poor sleeping habits and insomnia.
- an increased risk of self-harm.
- higher incidences of PTSD.

Perfectionism comes in different forms, though, and it can sometimes be tricky to identify whether or not you are merely a stickler for details or if you have blossomed into a fully-fledged perfectionist.

## THE TYPES OF PERFECTIONISM

Perfection has a couple of very distinct types, and while all of these types of perfectionism share the same behaviors, the motives differ.

Let's have a look at these types, how they differ, and how they affect our lives.

### Personal Standards Perfectionism

Personal standards perfectionism is probably the least damaging of the types of perfectionism we strive for, and this is purely because we set the standards for what motivates us.

Change our motivation and we change our standards—sounds simple enough, doesn't it?

If only!

Because our standards are rooted in our belief systems, we first need to change what we believe an adequate outcome is for ourselves.

The good news is that, when not extreme, personal standards of perfection are healthy for us and, most of the time, do not lead to burnout or stress.

When managed correctly, this type of perfectionism can actually help us cope with stress and strive to achieve our personal and professional goals. Personal standards perfectionism can, however, become self-critical, and this is when perfectionism becomes far more sinister.

### Self-Critical Perfectionism

When we set our goals too high or fear failure, perfectionism moves from personal standards to self-criticism.

Self-critical perfectionism often makes us feel hopeless and stops us from trying to do anything because we are afraid of making mistakes or not living up to our own or other people's standards.

Self-critical perfectionism is linked to avoidance, anxiety, and deep distress. Those of us who work in fields where excellence is expected are more likely to have this type of perfectionism.

Self-critical perfectionism is dangerous and has been shown to lead to higher incidences of self-harm and deep depression.

### Socially Prescribed Perfectionism

Cultural and societal standards can put enormous pressure on us to achieve loftily, and often ridiculously unrealistic, goals. Students are held to very high academic standards, not just by their parents but by teachers and their peers too.

Outside of schools, organizations are driving staff to achieve company goals that would have once been described as impossible, and with an endless line of new employees enthusiastically pursuing perfectionism, the pressure to succeed is enormous.

Added to this, social media often portrays idealistic lives and unfathomable wealth attained at a young age, creating more pressure for us to succeed at something that is not attainable for most.

## ARE YOU A PERFECTIONIST QUESTIONNAIRE

Still not sure whether or not you are obsessed with perfection?

Chances are that if any of what you have already read resonates with you, then perfectionism is at the very least banging persistently on the door of your psyche.

The fact that we live in an imperfect world probably doesn't mean much to you, and what little is written here about perfectionism hasn't done much to quell your fears about the unrealistic standards you are placing on yourself.

This perfectionism test, taken directly from Psychology Today, will help you to determine whether or not you have perfectionistic tendencies or if you have already fallen down the rabbit hole in pursuit of being perfect.

| Question | Strongly Agree | Agree | Might Agree or Disagree | Disagree | Strongly Disagree |
|---|---|---|---|---|---|
| Being average is the worst thing that could happen to me | | | | | |
| My work has to be perfect for me to be satisfied | | | | | |
| Failing an assignment or task means I am a failure | | | | | |
| I am only proud of my work if I am praised for it | | | | | |
| My life is littered with failures | | | | | |
| If I am not perfect my partner/family/ friends/ boss will reject me | | | | | |
| I don't like working with a team because things never get done properly | | | | | |
| If I make a mistake, it means I am incompetent | | | | | |
| It doesn't matter how hard I try I will never be good enough for others | | | | | |
| I find that I never have enough time to complete my tasks as I feel compelled to do things until they're perfect | | | | | |

| | | | | | |
|---|---|---|---|---|---|
| Satisfactory or average is never enough | | | | | |
| If my kids don't succeed, I am a failure | | | | | |
| I need to succeed at everything I do | | | | | |
| I believe that if I don't get it right the first time around then I have failed | | | | | |
| If I don't have a lot of money I cannot be respected | | | | | |
| My body needs to be in perfect shape or I will not be accepted by my partner or peer group | | | | | |
| I feel the need to point out other people's mistakes | | | | | |
| I have to be tough on my kids/friends/ family for them to be successful | | | | | |
| The prospect of making a mistake makes me feel anxious or stressed out | | | | | |

If you have answered "strongly agree" or 'agree' to more than half of these questions, chances are that you are being driven by perfection and should seek to rid yourself of the anxiety you're facing.

## THE INDECISION OVERVIEW

Perfectionism and indecision often go hand-in-hand, and for many of us, being torn between decisions can be as agonizing as pulling teeth.

Every single day, the human brain makes thousands of decisions, many of which we are never even aware of. These decisions are both big and small, and when some of us become aware that we need to make a decision, we can become stuck on something that should be small and insignificant.

Indecision is incredibly damaging—and I am not speaking about the big decisions like choosing your next career move either. Something as small as deciding whether or not to scramble, fry, or poach your eggs in the morning can lead you to waste hours wondering what the ramifications of your decision will be. If you are one of those people who just can't seem to make up their minds, you will know how frustrating and stressful it can be and what the deep psychological implications are for yourself.

I am by no means disputing the fact that this disposable, competitive world we live in is not filled with what most of us consider to be too many choices because it is. However, if you are finding yourself struggling to make even the smallest decisions, or if you are feeling overwhelmed and anxious about your impending decisions, you may be suffering from a deeply rooted fear of imperfection.

### *What Is Indecisiveness and What Does It Do to Our Mental Health?*

Indecisiveness is defined as the generalized difficulty of making satisfying decisions (Appel et al., 2021), and affects millions of people every single day.

For those of us who battle with being indecisive, this definition does not adequately explain the anxiety that having to weigh up the pros and cons of every option presents. Some of us experience indecisiveness so severe that we become paralyzed by the very thought of having to make a decision, and the "what ifs" of having to commit to anything can throw us into a deep depression as life, and opportunities pass us by.

That's not to say that we avoid making decisions entirely, but being satisfied with these decisions is another thing entirely.

For us to understand the impact of being indecisive, we first need to find the reasons why we are so indecisive in the first place, and only then can we examine the issues being indecisive can pose to our mental health.

While indecisiveness is not generally considered to be a psychiatric disorder, it can cross over into the realms of a disorder of aboulomania, and when this happens, it can affect our ability to function in our daily life.

Aboulomania hinders our ability to make any decision without feeling extreme anxiety, and regular indecisiveness impairs our ability to become successful.

Both of these conditions, aboulomania and generalized inde-cisiveness, are unhealthy ways to live, and when perfec-tionism is the driving force behind our indecisions, the psychological consequences can be devastating.

**Indecisiveness and Depression**

For those of us who have been struck down by depression, indecision is no stranger.

So why do we struggle with decisions when we are depressed?

The answer to that question is not as cut and dry as it seems, and everything from feeling that nothing matters, to being fearful that the decisions we make are not the right ones, can cause us to become depressed, which in turn, leads to further indecision.

Perhaps the biggest reason that indecision and depression go hand-in-hand is that dealing with the consequences of the decisions we make, especially when they don't pan out the way we had hoped, can lead us to feel negative emotions.

Avoidance of feeling any more doom and gloom than we already feel means decisions are risky for those of us with depression, and unfortunately, life doesn't come with the option of picking the winning box every single time. But we know for a fact that some boxes will be duds, and instead of lowering our expectations for perfection, we either avoid the boxes altogether or stand by idly, hoping that someone else will decide for us.

## Indecisiveness and Anxiety

Indecisiveness makes us feel anxious, and anxiety makes us feel indecisiveness. It sounds confusing, doesn't it?

Anxiety and indecisiveness are a two-way street that has us going backward and forward between the pros and cons of our choices. It's the equivalent of reversing to the end of your driveway only to put your vehicle back into drive, bringing it back up the driveway to its starting point over and over again.

Called double-sided regulation, anxiety, and indecision reside in communicating parts of the brain and as such, our anxiety eggs on our indecision, and our indecisions fuels our anxiety. As a result, our anxiety feeds on our indecision, which feeds on our anxiety.

When we feel anxious, it is near impossible to think straight, and we become less confident in our ability to evaluate the options available to us. All of this means we have the potential to get ourselves stuck in a loop of indecisiveness and anxiety that leads us down the road to depression as we find ourselves missing out on opportunities in our lives.

Anything from picking an option on a menu to larger decisions like buying a car or investing in property can trigger indecisiveness.

If you are undecided, or indecisive about whether or not you're indecisive, have a look at the quiz below.

## ARE YOU INDECISIVE QUIZ

| Question | Strongly Agree | Agree | Might Agree or Disagree | Disagree | Strongly Disagree |
|---|---|---|---|---|---|
| I find myself procrastinating a lot | | | | | |
| I can decide what to order off the menu easily | | | | | |
| I can entertain myself easily | | | | | |
| I just throw on whatever I want in the morning and go | | | | | |
| I feel intense anxiety if I am asked to lead a team | | | | | |
| I find it easier when others tell me what to do | | | | | |
| Working from home is not my forte and I never get anything done | | | | | |
| I find it difficult to follow a task through to completion | | | | | |
| I second guess myself often | | | | | |
| I am easily persuaded by what I read or see in the media | | | | | |

If you answered 'yes' or "strongly yes" to five or more of the questions above, you are indecisive. If you thought long and hard about how to answer these questions, you definitely have a problem with being indecisive.

## THE MAIN PERFECTIONISM AND INDECISION LINK

Perfectionists will find it difficult to make decisions because every decision needs to be well thought out in case the wrong decision leads to a mistake being made.

In extreme cases, the perfectionist may agonize over the smallest details and decisions, fearing that they will fall short of their own self-critical standards.

When we live in a constant state of anxiety over our decisions because we dread making mistakes, everything feels risky, but the truth is that we are being overly critical of ourselves.

If we allowed our mistakes to be reframed into learning experiences or saw our choices as a way to focus on the positive things, our choices would lead us to indecision, but then neither would perfectionism.

We need to learn that enough is not the mediocrity hook we hang our hats on. Rather, it is the standard we set for ourselves that we can reach. This way, we can learn from our mistakes and slowly, steadily, and reachably raise our goals.

For most of us, no single choice can ever lead to the catastrophic results we imagine they will lead to, and if they could, you are being presented with the wrong choices.

No one can achieve perfect results, not even if you feel that you have in the past, because if you look back and examine the process as well as the result, you will find that your idea of perfection has changed.

Perfection is a changeable ideology, and it doesn't exist.

### How Does Perfectionism Cause a Fear of Failure?

For some of us, the need to be perfect is paralyzing because we fear failure more than we fear ever even taking on a task or challenge.

If you fall into this category, you are not alone—some of the greatest achievers of our time have been crippled by their fear of failure or the fear that others would criticize or judge them.

Perfectionism is a pathological state that didn't even escape Steve Jobs, the creator of Apple. So strong was Jobs' need for perfection that he agonized over the perfect color of beige for his units and insisted on the internal components being as beautiful as the external facade of the product.

Jobs' perfection was so notorious that he was described as being almost tyrannical, and more than once, a product launch was stalled because the gadget didn't suit his perfectionistic standards.

Ultimately, Jobs' perfectionism got him fired from his position, even as a co-founder of the company, and it took.

For some of us, the need to be perfect is so strong that it leads to self-harm, and because perfectionists are often critical of themselves, depression and anxiety are almost unavoidable.

The mind of an achiever is set on being perfect, and if we want to get rid of the need to be perfect, we need to learn to be balanced and accept failure as much as we accept success.

Being an achiever doesn't mean you are not a perfectionist, and many of the greatest achievers known to mankind first had to free themselves from the web of perfectionism before they could truly become successful in life. You will have to learn to walk the thin line between perfecting your technique, keeping your technique, and taking action so that you can keep your mind and your creativity.

# 2

# THE ACHIEVER MINDSET

*Success in life is not for those who run fast, but for those who keep running and always on the move.*

— BANGAMBIKI HABYARIMANA

S uccessful people have a couple of characteristics in common, some of which make them high-achievers, but the most common of these traits is their mindset and a set of core beliefs.

Success means different things for different people, though, and some characteristics will apply to certain facets of our lives, while others will not. For example, being charismatic and extroverted is great for a motivational speaker but is not going to serve you particularly well as a neurosurgeon.

So, it makes more sense to figure out the achiever's core way of thinking than to look at their actual traits, though doing both can be helpful.

What is an achiever's mindset, though, and how can we learn from changing our mindset?

Before we dive into what mindset is required to become an achiever, we need to first look at the definition of mindset and what it means to us as perfectionists.

The definition of mindset is listed as, "1. a mental attitude or inclination" and "2. a fixed state of mind" (*Definition of MINDSET*, n.d.).

Let's break this definition down further, looking at what it means to have a perfectionist mindset and how that differs from an achiever's mindset.

When we have a perfectionist mindset, we believe that a task is not completed, or that it is not completed properly, unless it is flawless and perfect. This type of mindset is driven by a deep fear of failure, and it leads to procrastination, a lack of commitment, and depression. The perfectionist mindset is stuck in the process of achieving a task and how efficient or how exact these processes are. A stalled start is a perfectionist's best friend, and because of this, success rarely comes to us without agonizing over the smallest details. Alternatively, we may never even start a project without first being pressured into actually committing to a deadline.

An achiever's mindset, on the other hand, is one where the achiever sets a goal, analyzes, and commits to milestones before actioning their goal with precision targeting. But it is not just the action of these goals that creates an achiever mindset, or that just about anyone can set a lofty goal to achieve.

It is the passion, or the purpose of the achiever, that truly drives the achiever's mindset and a desire to achieve their end goal without fear of making mistakes or getting caught up in the details.

The achiever's why, or purpose, helps them to see past all of those scary obstacles some of us get caught up in, and the desire to stretch their boundaries to the limit that has them achieving their goals.

Does the achiever still feel fear?

Sure they do! But they also know that with proper preparation and action, their goals can be achieved.

Because of this, the achiever reframes their fear into excitement and an understanding that life is a journey filled with perfectly imperfect things—including them.

The largest difference between the achiever's mindset and the perfectionist's mindset is how they view tasks. The achiever always looks to the finishing line, putting one metaphorical foot in front of the other until they reach their goal. They do not get caught up in the process because they know that something will always come along to derail their plans, and that is okay because we have the choice of getting up and carrying on.

## WHY AN ACHIEVER MINDSET IS NECESSARY FOR SUCCESS

Perfectionists sometimes get trapped in the notion that success requires perfection and that without perfection, we cannot truly become successful.

The perfectionist's mindset is one that is fixed, driven by the fear of failure and a deep anxiety about having our inadequacies or weaknesses exposed. We become scared to try new things because we fear we will not do them correctly and mistakes are seen as fatal flaws, which prove we are just not good enough for the job, life, our relationship, etc.

A fixed mindset is one that has us stagnate, and no human does well when they do not grow.

We embrace mistakes as an opportunity to learn and are fueled by our passion and purpose. We strive for excellence purely through the happiness and satisfaction we feel when we have completed a task.

An achiever couldn't care less about approval or others making fun of their inadequacies because they know that by trying and failing, they will eventually achieve a result.

When we can learn to accept that challenges and mistakes are inevitable and that they will literally appear in every area of our lives, then we can teach ourselves a better way to approach the issues we are facing.

This leads me to the great conundrum any perfectionist faces —we don't want to make mistakes because it proves we are not perfect, and so we become stuck, rooted in place, hesitating for what feels like an eternity to ever start our lives.

Here's the thing about having a fixed, perfectionist mindset —it fools us into believing that once we become perfect, we will be successful, but the reality is that people with a growth, achiever mindset are far more likely to actually become successful (Dweck, 2015).

### Shifting From a Perfectionist Mindset to an Achiever Mindset

It can be hard to switch from focusing on perfection to focusing on achievement because we have to face our fears head-on and put them aside so we can get on with achieving.

Fear is a powerful driving force that has us acting irrationally—think about every horror film ever where the victim runs up the stairs, trapping themselves instead of running out of the door to freedom—and instead of finding ourselves behind a closed door with little option other than to scream hysterically, or jump out of the second-floor window, we need to stop, take a breath, and choose the next rational step to our freedom.

**Step 1:** Try something different when you are presented with an obstacle. That's right. You need to take a deep breath, get started, and when things don't work out, switch things up and try another angle to reach the end task.

**Step 2:** Let go of the goal of being perfect and focus on the goal of finishing. I'm not saying be sloppy with your work, but just get the task done and then look at how you can fine-tune it.

**Step 3:** Accept that perspective isn't fact and that it can be changed. Once your perspective changes, it becomes easier for you to see all of the opportunities available to you so that you can improve.

**Step 4:** Learn to learn! You're not going to grow if you don't first learn to become self-reflective and identify where things are going wrong for you. Sometimes our need for perfectionism comes from a place other than fear, but we will never know why we are being driven by perfectionism if we don't take the time to find out.

### *What Are the Characteristics of a High Achiever?*

Let's start with the obvious. Achievers are driven to achieve and become successful.

It is not just their deep desire to be successful that pushes them to achieve, though. Most achievers want to accomplish things that are meaningful to them.

The achiever is less preoccupied with avoiding failure and more focused on how they can be successful in a way that matters to them.

Always remember that success looks different to different people, and what matters to you may not matter to the next person. All of this means success is as subjective as your purpose, your beliefs, and your idea of what success looks like. It can grow, develop, and change as you do.

Before I continue with the characteristics of a high achiever, you must understand the difference between traits and characteristics.

Our traits are things we are born with and can help to distinguish us as different or as belonging to a group of other people with the same trait. In other words, I could be born with blue eyes; they distinguish me from the remainder of my family, who have green or brown eyes, but there are other people in the world with blue eyes. This trait makes me both unique and binds me to a community, and I cannot change the fact that I have blue eyes. Sure, I could wear contacts and pretend to have green or brown eyes, but at the end of the day, when those colored contacts come out, I still have blue eyes.

Characteristics, on the other hand, refer to our qualities. These qualities can be inherited or they can be learned over time as we interact with the world around us. Characteristics, therefore, are our behaviors and how we act from one moment to the next. For example, I was a very shy child in school and lacked the confidence to voice my opinion, so I joined a public speaking club and learned to overcome my shyness through tenacity and determination. Today, I am a public speaker, delivering my messages of success to packed auditoriums. Tenacity and determination are traits of mine, but they weren't always present and I had to learn these skills.

Now that you know the difference between characteristics and traits, let's examine the characteristics of achievers.

## Characteristic 1: Action-Orientated

The high achiever doesn't have time to mess around and procrastinate. They take aim and fire, getting out of the starting blocks quickly.

The perfectionist takes their time and chooses to get ready before taking aim. Sometimes, getting ready and aiming wears them out so much that they don't have the energy to even take the shot.

Taking aim and firing several shots will have the high achiever hit the target at least once, and when they're done with target practice, they can assess how to become more accurate, figuring out how things work as they go along.

Both the high achiever and the perfectionist have the same intention when taking the shot, but the perfectionist either never fires or only fires once in the hope of hitting the bullseye.

And look, it's great that we can talk a good game, but the world needs action-oriented people who walk the talk.

Will you get it right every time?

Absolutely not, but you will have a better chance of actually becoming great at something because you are allowing yourself the opportunity to fine-tune your skills.

**Characteristic 2: Vision**

I am not disputing that perfectionists do have a vision, but their vision is often focused on every small detail instead of stepping back and taking a look at the bigger picture.

Is a mosaic just as beautiful with a few missing pieces?

Do we even notice the missing pieces when we step back to view the mosaic for what it is?

No... So, why do we get caught up in making sure everything is perfect when no one will even notice something is amiss? Heck! Sometimes the missing pieces actually add charm and character to the piece, making it even more beautiful.

High achievers are able to take that step back and see what the overall picture looks like in their minds before they begin to lay the tiles of the artwork of their lives. They can see what it feels like, what they will do, and how they will put each of these pieces together before coming back to the present and acting on their vision.

You must build a clear vision of what you want so that you have a defined pathway to walk on, but also so that you have the passion and drive to walk around the obstacles that may crop up on your path.

A clear destination or a vision that you can live, feel, breathe, and work every single day is the single most important tool a high achiever has. It is the driving force behind them achieving their goals and the reason they get up every morning to tackle the day's tasks.

**Characteristic 3: Focus**

There is an old saying that says, "if you chase two rabbits, you will catch none," and the perfectionist is certainly guilty of chasing far too many variables when trying to achieve their goals.

The achiever knows what they want to achieve and goes for it with laser focus because they know that the risk of losing focus is not achieving their goals.

Without focusing on the end goal, all you will ever achieve is an endless list of what ifs and a maze of rabbit burrows that will have you lost while the rabbit sits in the open, mocking you for being buried underground while they are freely available to be caught.

When we come to think of it, everyone has the ability to or certainly has dreamed of big ideas, but few of us actually make these dreams a reality, and the reason for this is a lack of focus in achieving what we have dreamed. Always remember, where focus goes, energy flows.

## Characteristic 4: Discipline

Discipline is the act of consistently getting up, showing up, and acting on the milestones required to achieve our goals.

It is the understanding that consistent performance over time will help us achieve what we have set as a goal, and it shows commitment—a characteristic that is far more sought after than perfection.

Between our goals and our accomplishments is a gap, and discipline is the bridge that closes the gap between our ideas or dreams and achieving these goals and dreams.

The difference between a high achiever and a perfectionist is the ability to consistently chip away at the obstacles they are facing, as opposed to giving up because they haven't got it quite right.

High achievers are in the driver's seat of their lives, and they do not leave the end destination to chance. They learn to build small habits that plot a route and eventually gain momentum so that they can arrive at their goals.

Self-discipline is probably the toughest skill people need to learn because we believe we need to change everything for us to make a difference, when you just need to make a promise to yourself to change one small thing every day that will help you move closer to your goal and your dreams.

**Characteristic 5: Can-Do Attitude**

The high achiever has a positive attitude that values determination and the need to succeed.

These are the people who don't see obstacles as scary, but rather as challenges that can be overcome. They're less worried about what they can't do and more focused on what they can't.

We all have a choice in life: To be the victor or the victim, and it's not our circumstances that create our success but our attitude.

- Victors have a sense of purpose that makes them look into their future and decide that they will get things done so that they can live their future.
- Victors see mistakes as opportunities to learn, not as a reason to stop pursuing their dreams.
- Victors play to win—they never even contemplate losing.
- Victors choose to do hard things because they know nothing great comes from the path of least resistance.

- Victors take ownership of their failures and their successes. They relish a challenge because they know it is an opportunity to build their resilience.

High achievers make sure that they take responsibility for their lives, their goals, their purpose, and their aspirations, turning their dreams into goals and their goals into reality.

Challenge 6: A Passion for Learning

The high achiever understands that anyone can do anything they want to do if they learn how to.

The world is an extremely competitive place, and if we are going to continue to achieve in our lives, we need to learn how to overcome our weaknesses.

High achievers value education because they know that moving forward is the only way to be successful. Added to this, they know that the best version of themselves is the one who embraces every opportunity to experience life, learn, and feed their minds on a personal and professional level.

## Characteristic 7: Positive Contributors

High achievers may be relentless in their pursuit of success, but that doesn't mean they are selfish in their achievements.

The value of helping others, making a positive difference in other people's lives, and gaining a deeper insight into how others think, what their struggles are, and how they are overcoming them.

Sharing contributions with other people helps the high achiever to experience life from other people's points of view and allows them to be empathetic in their journey to success.

Like with everything else in life, there are pros and cons to choosing a specific mindset, and choosing to be a high achiever is no different.

## THE INS AND OUTS OF A HIGH ACHIEVER

Have you ever seen the movie, *"Men of Honor,"* starring Cuba Gooding Jr and Robert de Niro?

If you haven't, do yourself a favor and watch it for all of its tear-jerking, high-achieving, determination-driven qualities.

The young Carl Brashear refuses to give up, and achieves better than everyone in his master diver's class, despite having to face enormous challenges and obstacles in his quest to become the best navy diver the United States Navy had ever seen.

Brashear, played by Gooding Jr., shows a level of tenacity and drive that so many perfectionists could learn from because he makes mistakes along the way but never allows these mistakes to stop him from achieving his goal of becoming a master diver.

As with many things, film imitates real life a lot of the time, and while *"Men of Honor"* certainly is a powerful reminder of why perfectionism doesn't necessarily equate to achievement, it also shows us that being a high achiever comes with a set of pros and cons.

### The Pros of Being a High Achiever

High achievers are filled with pride and a sense of satisfaction in whatever they do. High achievers value success in all areas of their life, and as such, they place pride in everything they do.

While too much pride can be damaging, taking pride in what we do and how we do it can be a great motivator for us to achieve our goals, regardless of whether or not they are personal or professional.

This sense of pride almost always carries over to the high achiever's family, and when the high achiever balances their work and family lives, the high achiever can instill a sense of pride, and a great work ethic in the people they value the most too.

High achievers are usually organized, with a clear and definitive roadmap to their goals and future success, but they also consider any obstacles they may encounter, and plan for these. All of this leads to lower stress levels for the high achiever, and the ability to understand that some days they may have to work more so that other days they can work less helps the high achiever to keep their stress in check.

Finally, the high achiever develops more long-term business and personal relationships. The reason for this is that people are drawn to steadfast, disciplined characters; it makes them feel safe, and because they know the high achiever produces consistent results every time, they will keep coming back to the high achiever.

### The Cons of Being a High Achiever

Before we look at the cons of being a high achiever, it is important that you know that when achievement bleeds into perfectionism, issues occur.

There are no real cons to being a true high achiever, but there are cons to being a high achiever who has perfectionistic tendencies.

Perhaps the most significant issue that a high achiever faces is anxiety, as well as the demands of long hours and the pressure to succeed. High achievers are always on the edge between excitement and stress, and a lot of the time, the human brain simply doesn't know how to differentiate between being excited and being just plain stressed out. Because of this, it is important that the high achiever looks out for signs of stress and anxiety and that they nip stress in the bud before it causes anxiety issues.

Another issue that high achievers face is developing a long list of unhealthy habits in order to train and sustain their energy levels, reduce anxiety, and maintain their attention span.

When high achievers begin to push themselves into perfectionism, they can force themselves to work long hours, drink too much coffee or caffeine, neglect their mental and physical health, and may even forget to eat.

Lastly, high achievers can tend to work too much, and this means missing out on the right moment.

Focusing on future goals is great, but losing sight of what is happening today can cause the high achiever to feel anxious.

It is vital that we live in the present because the present is where we take the actions required to achieve our goals.

## THE PERFECTIONIST VS. THE HIGH ACHIEVER

When we want every task, person, room, or even area of our life to be exactly how we imagined, it can leave us feeling a little bit anxious, emotional, and even out of sync with the world—an understatement, I know... But when all of these things fall short, it just becomes too much and the feeling that you or other people could have done better takes over.

For us to feel good about what we have accomplished because things didn't work out perfectly seems a little ridiculous, but for the perfectionist, living with these feelings is an everyday reality.

If you can identify with any of the feelings or expectations mentioned above, then there is a real chance that you are a perfectionist, and while being a perfectionist certainly comes with a whole lot of amazing attributes and even rewards, it is also downright exhausting.

My own journey to freeing myself from perfectionism led me to believe that there wasn't much difference between a perfectionist and a high achiever, but one critical characteristic was glaringly obvious in its difference—the motivation, or driving force, behind these two types of people.

Both the perfectionist and the high achiever want one thing above everything else; to succeed. But the perfectionist is motivated by fear of failing, while the achiever is motivated by the success of succeeding.

Confused?

Let me simplify it even further—the perfectionist is driven to succeed, and the high achiever has the drive to succeed.

When we look at that statement deeper, the perfectionist is in the passenger seat, going along for the ride called life, and the achiever is in the driver's seat, steering their way to the life they want.

### The Perfectionist Under the Microscope

Perfectionists are driven by the fear of failure and rejection. They do things because of a deep fear of rejection or of being ridiculed, and it is this fear that tends to lower their self-esteem.

Being a perfectionist means seeking validation from outside sources, and the perfectionist hasn't yet learned how to find inner acceptance and self-validation. This leads them to have a dogged determination (as with the high achiever), but for different reasons, and the perfectionist will get so bogged down in the most minute of details that they forget to enjoy the journey they are on.

Added to all of this, the perfectionist is all about the world being black or white, and this makes it very difficult for the perfectionist to think outside of the box when it comes to issues they may face. This rigidity in thinking can also mean the perfectionist takes criticism especially harshly, losing confidence, and even questioning their abilities when anyone criticizes them.

### The High Achiever Under the Microscope

High achievers strive to do their best, not be perfect, with everything they take on in life. They do not expect others to meet their standards and understand that everyone is on their own journey to success.

The high achiever knows that mistakes are inevitable and they embrace these mistakes, never allowing failures or upset to discourage them from the end goal. It is the high achiever's resilience in confronting and overcoming weaknesses that ensures they learn from every step of their personal journey.

Unlike perfectionists, high achievers value constructive criticism, seeing it as another opportunity to grow and better themselves through the opinions and advice of others. High achievers may also feel stress from time to time, but they value the journey to success so much that this stress is mostly short-lived. Plus, high achievers will have learned how to deal with the stress they encounter along the way.

While it is true that perfectionists and high achievers have a lot of common characteristics, it is often their mindsets and their motivation that set them apart.

All of this is good news for perfectionists, though, because if a perfectionist can train their minds to make these two small changes, they can easily let go of the fear of failure, embracing a new way of life.

### Some Things for a Perfectionist to Ponder On

For you to become a high achiever and leave your perfectionism days behind you, there are a few things you will need to tweak.

I know criticism is not your strong point, but I implore you to look at these points as a way to unbind yourself from the shackles you are currently lugging around with you. I can only provide you with the keys to these shackles, though, and it is still entirely up to you to use the tools provided to you so that you can finally be free to succeed in life.

1. Learn to become at peace with who you are so that you will no longer be driven by the fear of not being liked, accepted, or acknowledged. Yes, you may not have a whole lot of people who will understand your sudden shift in viewpoint, but I promise you that once you find your way, people will learn to value your tenacity and new driving force far more than you being a stickler for details.

2. Start to think before you act in fear, because when it comes down to it, society will never value you as much as you think they do. Very few people make it into the history books for being a perfectionist, not with good stories in any case, so learn to become enamored with you and your journey. At the end of your life, the only thing that will matter to you is that you lived your years on this planet happy and within your personal definition of success.

3. Do yourself a favor and say no as often as you possibly can. Perfectionists are taken advantage of by people who don't want to commit to doing a task properly or those who don't want to see things through. You can say 'No' respectfully but say it nonetheless—you'll thank yourself later! Your efforts need to be focused on your goals and not achieving the goals of people who are too lazy to get up and chase their own success.

4. Stop multitasking; at least for now, because you will need to learn to focus on the goals you have set for

yourself. When shifting from perfectionist to high achiever, it is vitally important that you do not split your focus because you are retraining your brain to do the best you can do, not a million tasks perfectly at once.

5. Start being gentle with yourself and others as you learn to embrace your mistakes. Being a perfectionist also means being difficult to live with, work with, and socialize with—it's even difficult to live with ourselves. Understand that life is about making healthy, loving, and supportive relationships where people respect our evolution through life, our boundaries, and our standards. This point ties in strongly with point 3, learning to say no because we are so readily taken advantage of.

6. Embrace failure right now, because becoming a high achiever means making a lot of mistakes. You're going to problem-solve and laugh off a lot of bizarre things you uncover about yourself. You'll run into a lot of problems and roadblocks on your journey, but the good things that come out of your mistakes will be much better than anything you've ever done as a perfectionist.

Training yourself to step out of being a perfectionist is not going to be easy, but once you realize how you can put your high standards to good use, your quality of life will improve exponentially.

### *High Achievers Who Have Failed*

Before high achievers achieve success, they must first learn how to become successful.

Some of the most successful people in the world have failed at least once. While we celebrate their success, we often forget about their journeys and the steps they took to get where they are now.

Success is a path that is marked by failure, and without these failures, the high achievers listed below would probably never have reached their goals.

### Rowan Atkinson

Rowan Atkinson is one of Britain's most well-known comedy actors, but acting is not his only accomplishment.

Atkinson first obtained a degree in Electrical Engineering from Newcastle University. It was only when Atkinson applied to do his Master's degree at Oxford University that the now well-known actor became known for his comedy and acting.

Rowan Atkinson is the perfect example of how the choices we make for ourselves are not always the right ones, and that when we are driven by our passion, as well as a need to try out every opportunity that comes our way, we can become successful in our lives.

## Lily Cole

British actress and model Lily Cole is proof that super-models can be intelligent, and after performing incredibly well in her A-levels, she was offered a place at King's College, where she started studying History of Art.

Cole was one of seven people in her year to achieve a First-Class Honors, the highest honors classification for British university students. Later, Cole would also receive a double First-Class.

What is remarkable about this accomplishment is that Cole was able to do this all while being an international super-model and sought-after actress.

Lily Cole is the perfect example of how passion, determination, and organization can drive a person to success.

## Clare Balding

Sports presenter Clare Balding was the President of the Cambridge Union Society, an amateur jockey, and graduated before beginning her broadcasting career.

She has been named one of the United Kingdom's top 100 most influential women and continues to be a high achiever in everything she sets her mind to.

Balding is proof that if you stay focused and allow yourself to be open to new opportunities, and approach these opportunities with a can-do attitude.

## Steve Jobs

We have already discussed Jobs a little bit. The now infamous founder of Apple was fired from his job at Apple. He proceeded to fail at the two companies he founded after Apple until he was asked to come back to Apple, which was in absolute disarray.

Today, Apple is one of the most successful companies in the United States of America. Jobs demonstrates that when a perfectionist channels their tendencies correctly, they can achieve great success.

## Steven Spielberg

Spielberg was turned down twice for film school, even though he is now one of the most well-known directors of all time and has won many prestigious awards.

He didn't give up on his dream, though, and through sheer tenacity and determination, Spielberg has become arguably one of the most successful directors of our time. Years after his initial rejection from the school that rejected him, Spielberg received an honorary degree as a token of appreciation for his contribution to film.

Steven Spielberg is proof that determination will open more doors for you than any degree ever will.

## Bill Gates

Not only did Bill Gates drop out of Harvard, but his first company tanked.

Gates, unwavering in his beliefs, tapped into self-discipline, persevering every time his business ideas were rejected. His perseverance and dedication to his dreams led Gates to become the youngest self-made millionaire in history through his company, Microsoft.

Gates is well-known for his motivational speeches in which he praises failures as the greatest lessons he has ever learned.

Bill Gates and his ex-wife Melinda would also become some of the greatest philanthropists in modern history.

Gates shows that failure is not the end of the world and that we can be successful if we learn from our mistakes.

## Stephen King

King was a deeply troubled child who was raised in poverty and with no father figure. When he was a child, King witnessed his friend's tragic death, although he denies any memory of the event.

The public, however, believes that this event would later become King's inspiration for some of his much darker works.

King took on a whole lot of jobs while trying to get through college, including working as a janitor. To supplement his income, he sold short stories to a men's magazine.

Eventually, King's novel, Carrie, was accepted by a publishing house, and the rest, as they say, is history.

Steven King is a testament to the fact that our history should have no bearing on our endeavors, and that when we don't give up on our dreams and we act on our goals, anything is possible.

## THE ACTION STEPS TO BECOMING A HIGH ACHIEVER

When we look at the examples of high achievers above, it becomes clear that for you to shift from perfectionism to high achiever, you will need to take a couple of steps.

Passion and perseverance are a must for us to become a high achiever in the long term.

For the perfectionist, though, a sustainable effort is terrifying, though, because being perfect all of the time is just plain exhausting!

Before you even begin with the steps below, it is important that you let go of every idea you have that perfectionism is the only way to become a high achiever. By remaining stuck in your perfectionist tendencies, you have less chance of becoming a high achiever.

Now that we've dispelled the myth that perfectionism is required to be a high achiever, let's look at the critical steps for shifting your perfectionism mindset to an achiever mindset.

### Step 1: Find Your Purpose

You need to find your purpose in life first and foremost.

What is important to remember is that your purpose is not a label—if you're an author, what is your purpose? Are you a storyteller?... An educator? Finding your purpose will make it easier for you to become more motivated to achieve your goals.

The purpose is what gets you up in the morning and will give you the grit you need to keep going when things get hard.

Having an understanding of what motivates us can be difficult though, and for a lot of us, the reason we are perfectionistic in the first place is that we are not working within our purpose, and so we simply don't have the motivation to follow through with our goals.

You need to start with your why, which means finding not just the label we place on our motivators, but actually finding what sets our soul on fire. Oprah Winfrey, for example, has always named her purpose as an educator. In fact, to this day, she credits her passion, drive, and success to the fact that she wanted to teach people, and without a doubt, she is teaching and has taught millions of people around the world.

Finding your purpose is a very hard-to-define goal, and if you haven't got a clue where to begin, start by identifying what your values are.

Once you know this, you can align your goals to your values, and always remember to set small goals first so that you can build on your self-discipline for those larger goals later on.

### Step 2: Be Passionate

Passion will be the fuel you put on the fire of your motivation and your goals. Passion is your ambition—and as you know, you already have plenty of ambition but just don't know how to apply it correctly.

High achievers almost always use their underlying passion to hone in on their goals, especially when things get tough, and the best part about passion is that it is contagious. When you can find the passion inside you and apply this passion to your goals, then others around you will be more likely to support you and help to motivate you toward your goals.

Instead of getting stuck in perfectionism, choose to stop and ask yourself, "Why do I want to be a high achiever?" and then use that answer to become passionate about your goals.

### *Step 3: Practice!*

Once you have your passion and purpose locked in, you can practice achieving your goals.

Set small goals and practice completing these goals until you have formed the habits required to set larger goals for yourself.

I'm not going to lie to you; setting lofty goals takes a whole lot of effort, and to become good at setting goals and achieving them, you need to practice a whole lot!

Because high achievers don't leave their lives and their goals up to anyone else, they understand that practicing both their strengths and their weaknesses needs to be done so that they can move forward a little bit every day toward being the high achiever they want to be.

Being a high achiever means following through with what you start, committing to getting the task done, and not getting it done perfectly.

You will need to make peace with the fear of impending rejection because failure is inevitable in life, and as you now know, it doesn't mark the end of your journey to success.

Commit to being in charge of your own life, and remove your fate from the hands of perfectionism so that you can get better at pursuing your goals every day. Be deliberate in your actions, and push yourself on the days you just don't feel like doing what needs to be done.

Set stretch goals along with your small goals. Setting a stretch goal is one in which we choose to set a goal outside of what we are comfortable with usually achieving. What stretch goals do for us is force ourselves outside of our comfort zones.

Find a mentor that will help to motivate you when you feel like you are stepping too far outside of your comfort zone. Once you have achieved a stretch goal, it becomes far easier to see exactly how amazing you truly are and how capable you are of achieving great things.

### Step 4: Become Courageous

High achievers are not only brave in their beliefs but also in the way they go after their goals.

You have to come to terms with the fact that the world is a very competitive place and that you will face your fair share of rejection.

Rejection, however, does not mean you are a failure, and knowing that the odds are stacked in your favor of failing a lot helps you to know where to start and when to have the courage to get up, dust yourself off, and keep pushing forward.

Courage is an essential component of becoming a high achiever, and the first step to becoming courageous is to manage your fear of failure.

High achievers, in fact, have learned that failure and rejection are nothing more than opportunities to grow and understand the valuable lessons that can be learned with every single setback they face.

It's important that you learn to become introspective so that you can manage and reframe your negative beliefs and thoughts. Stop comparing yourself to other people, because your journey is uniquely yours. Instead, choose to be mindful, learn to be organized, and brush off rejection when you're presented with it.

### Step 5: Learn the Art of Perseverance

Pursuing any long-term goal is about having the perseverance to overcome the struggles, setbacks, and challenges you will inevitably encounter.

The bottom line is that life is full of hardships and it comes with a whole lot of roadblocks. As a perfectionist, when you are faced with potential failure, you choose to throw in the proverbial towel, choosing to move on to something you are good at rather than keeping on keeping on.

High achievers choose to get up and carry on regardless of the roadblock they encounter, choosing to find an alternative route to achieve their goals.

It's important that you keep going no matter what happens, and instead of throwing your hands in the air, loudly proclaiming the world is against you, you need to fix things yourself.

Mel Robbins, a motivational speaker, puts it best when she says, *"No one is coming to save you."* The world owes you nothing, and it will take perseverance, strength, and sheer determination to overcome the obstacles you are facing.

You will need to take action by identifying which goals are worthy of your passion and perseverance. Make sure your goals are visible so that you can use your emotions to drive your behaviors toward a positive outcome.

### Step 6: Learn to Be Resilient

One more time, a little louder for those of you at the back.

Life is going to present you with some pretty nasty surprises along the way, and for you to continue to pursue your goals despite these surprises, you will need to learn to be resilient in the face of adversity.

Your ability to withstand stress and other emotional experiences will allow you to get back up when life knocks you down and will have you put one step in front of the other even if you are rejected or have failed.

Learning to be resilient also means learning how to combine your creativity with confidence and adding a touch of optimism.

Being resilient will help you to become realistically optimistic about your chances to succeed, even when the odds are stacked against you. It gives you confidence in your skills so that you can keep going after your goals.

When the world rejects you, which it inevitably will, resilience is what will give you the edge, helping you to resist the urge to return to your old ways.

To become resilient, you should start by looking for opportunities that help you get to know yourself better. Opportunities for self-discovery provide a unique opportunity to change your perspective on your ability to do difficult things, even when you believe you cannot.

Realistically speaking, everyone, even the highest of achievers, has encountered roadblocks in their life, but it is the steps above that have had them stare adversity in the eye, choosing to go for their goals regardless.

Having said that, you will need to be patient with yourself because it takes time to build up the grit you need to become a high achiever.

## THE HIGH ACHIEVER'S HABIT CHECKLIST

Our habits can either hurt us or help us, and while bad habits certainly do get most of the limelight when it comes to why we cannot achieve what we set out to do, good habits are what we should be focusing on.

When we choose to replace our bad habits with good ones, we can live a life that is filled with learning, achievements, and rewards. The high achiever is focused on the results they will achieve, and this helps to motivate them to keep moving toward their goals.

This determination to achieve the goals we set out for ourselves first starts with the habits we choose to form.

Below is a high achievers habit list.

I would suggest that you print this list out and tick off each of the items on it every day.

This way, you can keep track of your daily high achiever habits, and after 66 days, the number of days psychology says it takes to form a habit, you will be well on your way to becoming a high achiever (Clear, 2014).

| Habit | Mon | Tue | Wed | Thur | Fri | Sat | Sun |
|---|---|---|---|---|---|---|---|
| Try a new pattern–figure out when your most productive time is by working at different times | | | | | | | |
| Schedule time for thought or meditation | | | | | | | |
| Plan every day with SMART goals that you can achieve | | | | | | | |
| Do one thing that makes you uncomfortable | | | | | | | |
| Exercise every day–a healthy body is a healthy mind | | | | | | | |
| Read for 30 minutes–make sure you are sticking to self-development topics | | | | | | | |
| Journal your gratitude for the day | | | | | | | |
| Be curious once a day–explore one different thing that interests you every day | | | | | | | |
| Ask yourself an open-ended question and explore where it takes you | | | | | | | |
| Get better sleep–create a great sleep hygiene routine so that you can get quality sleep | | | | | | | |

Being a perfectionist and being a high achiever are not too different. It is our habits and our ability to commit to completing a task that will help us to shift from perfectionism to achievement.

Learning how to turn inward and deal with our inner critical voice will help us to make the changes we need to make so that we can shift our rear into gear, driving ourselves to success.

# 3

# FINDING YOUR INNER VOICE

A couple of years ago, a friend of mine was training for a cycle race. He had purchased a brand new bike in anticipation of the race, and on the first Saturday after his purchase, he decided to take his bike out for a spin.

I happened to call him as he was clipping his water bottle into the newly installed drink holder, and among the idle chit-chat between friends, he said to me, "I don't know if I should go out this morning. Something feels off."

I suggested that he shouldn't go, especially if he had a bad feeling about his impending ride, before wishing him well and hanging up.

A couple of hours later, I got a call from my friend's wife. Confused, I answered, a sick feeling in my gut that something had happened, especially since there had been an ominous tone to the earlier telephone conversation.

My friend had had an accident and was in surgery to repair the damage to his battered body.

Upon arriving at the hospital, I was told that my friend was lucky to have only suffered a broken leg, and as relieved as I was that nothing more serious had happened, I couldn't help but think that he would not have been in that hospital if he had trusted his inner voice.

We've heard the sayings so often, "Trust your gut, go with your instincts, or follow your intuition," but there aren't very many of us that actually know what that means.

The external noise we are drowned in, as well as the internal conflict we are constantly battling, often drowns out our inner voices, silencing the inner wisdom we all have. We talk ourselves out of what our inner voice says, but the fact of the matter is that when we choose to listen to our inner voice, decision-making is far easier.

So, how do we listen to our inner voice, especially when it is competing with all of the other noise, and what exactly is our inner voice?

## WHAT IS YOUR INNER VOICE?

People call their inner voice several things—their gut, insight, and innate wisdom.

The dictionary defines our inner voice as "the ability to understand something immediately, without the need for conscious reasoning" (Merriam-Webster Dictionary, 2022).

For most of us, our inner voice is known as our intuition, and it is a sometimes loud and annoying feeling that tells us right and wrong, and sometimes it is a whisper that is barely audible.

When we learn to listen to our inner voice or intuition, making snap decisions and judgments becomes so much easier.

Numerous studies by cognitive neuroscientists have shown that only 5% of our decision-making, emotions, behaviors, and actions come from our conscious mind, with a startling 95% of our brain activity happening on a subconscious level (van Gaal et al., 2012).

Our brains take in information all the time, utilizing our senses to process our environment and situation at mind-blowing (pardon the pun) speed. This means your hunch or intuition is being sent to you out of masses of information that you aren't even aware of.

### But What About Cognition?

Well, cognition is the conscious, 5% part of our brain that is used to understand, problem-solve, and organize our lives. It is the part of our brain that controls logical thoughts, and while it is great to have, it is also responsible for overriding our intuition most of the time.

Cognition is what has us weighing up the pros and cons of any situation and has us coming to a rational conclusion based on the input of data that is received from our senses and the information stored in our brain.

We call this our voice of reason, and yes, it works, but it can silence our intuition if we let it.

### I Don't Have an Inner Voice

If I had a dime for every time someone told me they didn't have an inner voice, I would be wealthy.

Here's the thing, your inner voice isn't always a voice, it's not always in your head, and it certainly isn't always apparent, especially if you have learned to silence it.

For some people, their inner voice is more of a feeling, an image, or even a sensation. It is not so much a voice as it is an energy or motion that they feel that says this feels good, I am excited, don't do that, or run for the hills right now!

No one way of experiencing your inner voice is correct, just like there is no one correct way to experience our thoughts. What is important is that you learn to identify what your intuition is for you and where specifically you feel it.

There is a reason intuition is known by many names, and that is because people feel it and listen to it differently. From your heart to your head, and even your gut, your intuition is there—you just need to pay attention and find it.

## INNER CONFIDENCE, YOUR INNER VOICE, AND SUCCESS

You may be asking, "Why does intuition matter?" And "why am I rambling about your inner voice and intuition?" Especially when this book is about overcoming perfectionism.

Remember when I mentioned your inner critic?

Your inner voice, whether you hear it or not, not only helps us to make decisions, but it is also what drives your behaviors.

What about cognition? Well, it also helps us to make decisions and drives our behaviors, but in a different way.

Let's break these two concepts down so that you can better understand the difference.

Our inner voice is what builds our confidence. It works with all of the information we have received over the years to help make spot decisions. When we make decisions that work out for us, our inner voice stores this information and uses it to help us make future great decisions. It also helps to boost our confidence and ensures we become confident in our ability to not only make decisions but to follow through with them to a positive outcome.

Cognition, on the other hand, is conscious and it weighs up the pros and cons of the situations we are presented with. It is the voice of praise, or criticism, that we hear, or feel, once we have made our decisions. Cognition is responsible for most of our talking ourselves out of doing certain things and is almost always driven by fear.

So, what does this have to do with being a perfectionist?

Perfectionists are stuck with what they know. They constantly weigh the pros and cons of every choice we make and criticize the choices we made in the past that didn't work out.

For us to build inner confidence, it would make sense that we need to learn to listen to our intuition and silence our inner critic or listen to our inner voice to a point before we close our eyes and just commit.

### Why Is Inner Confidence a Must for Success

Inner confidence, also known as self-confidence, is linked to happiness and living a life that is successful and fulfilling.

Being confident is linked with self-reward, the most prominent driving force behind highly successful people.

These benefits include less anxiety and ridding ourselves of the fear that drives our perfectionistic behaviors, greater motivation to pursue our goals, more resilience, and a stronger sense of our purpose.

Let's break down each of these self-rewards in greater detail and look at how to build our confidence, as well as learn to change our inner critic into an inner cheerleader.

## Reduced Anxiety and Fear

The more confident we become, the easier it will be for you to calm your inner critic, or tell it to shut up!

With confidence, we can take a moment to listen to our intuition, changing our inner dialogue from "I can't do it" to "I can do anything!"

Inner confidence allows us to unplug from our thoughts and take action that is in line with our values and our purpose.

When we suffer from low self-confidence we ruminate on our decisions, mulling over all of the things that worry us and imagining all of the mistakes we could make if we do take action.

The issue with excessively ruminating over our thoughts and the decisions we need to make is that it causes depression and anxiety and forces us to withdraw from the world as we fight our fear of making a mistake.

Inner confidence is one of the few ways we can stop overthinking and quiet our inner critics at the same time.

## Greater Motivation

When we want to feel more confident, we take small, meaningful steps that help us have a positive conversation with ourselves.

Taking these small, meaningful steps helps us to see that we can not only overcome setbacks but also do hard things outside of our comfort zones.

Being a perfectionist, you probably already know that the 'A' you got in calculus back in high school made you feel proud, but it didn't do anything to help build your inner confidence now, did it?

What you really have to ask yourself is if this accomplishment was easy for you, or if you had to persevere to make sure you got that A? And if you did persevere, where did you lose that confidence?

Triumphing over adversity, or achieving that A was probably done through the small steps you took, and for you to become successful in other areas of your life, you need to cast aside self-doubt and allow your confidence to blossom and grow.

The first few steps will, without a doubt, be difficult, but once you gain momentum, those thoughts of "what if" will begin to diminish.

When we lose confidence in our abilities, we need to prove to ourselves that we can still take the steps needed to become high-achieving individuals. Also, taking small steps lets us focus on achieving our goals instead of letting our fears of failure and being imperfect hold us back.

## More Resilience

Once we start to gain momentum and confidence in our abilities, we start to see setbacks for what they are instead of a reason to quit because we're scared of failure.

Having inner confidence certainly does not mean you will never fail, because you will, but you will have enough confidence in yourself to try again rather than throw the towel in.

You will know that you can try as many times as you want, especially when things don't work out the way you want them to, and you can avoid beating yourself up for the mistakes you have made while learning.

Confidence also drives you to try new things, and by doing this, you will finally understand how failure and the mistakes you make are actually beneficial to your personal growth.

Failure, as you now know, is a part of life, and when we are more willing to fail, we actually open ourselves up to more opportunities to succeed.

Self-confidence ensures we don't wait until everything is 100 percent ready for us to act—we learn to take a whole lot of shots at goal so that at least one of these shots hits the center of the hoop.

## A Strong Sense of Purpose

Inner confidence allows us to explore who we truly are and lets us come to terms with all of our strengths and weaknesses.

We begin to understand that neither our strengths nor our weaknesses define us and that, by working on ourselves, we can become strong at whatever we put our mind to.

Finding our sense of purpose also allows us to celebrate our journey to success rather than berating ourselves for the things we have missed out on because of our perfectionism.

Once our confidence begins to soar, we will begin to work and live within our principles and our purpose, which will ignite our passion and drive us to success.

Knowing who we are is the single greatest gift we can give to ourselves because working with purpose helps us to speak up, stand up, and show up in our own lives.

Inner confidence is a must for success because it allows us to let our best selves shine through, and lets us know that being perfectly imperfect is absolutely fine.

### The Types of Inner Voices

Research suggests that, on average, we speak to ourselves for 23% of our day.

People who have a heightened sense of awareness can actually speak to themselves a whole lot more than that, and people who have no self-awareness can actually be devoid of an inner voice, or more accurately, they are not aware of their inner voice.

Your inner voice can be divided into a monologue, in which you tell yourself something but not with the intention of having a conversation, and a dialogue, where you actually converse with yourself as if someone or something else is in your brain.

Aside from these monologues and dialogues, we have five categories of internal experiences:

- inner speech
- mental imagery
- feelings
- sensory awareness
- unsymbolized thinking, and mentalizing

Each of these internal experiences plays a critical role in how we think and can be manipulated with the use of external symbolism.

However, not everyone hears a voice, and internal monologue and dialogue can vary greatly, with some people seeing images, others seeing numbers or graphs, and still others hearing music or bursts of color that they associate with any of the five experiences listed above.

For example, people who are hearing impaired will experience their inner voice through images that they sign to themselves as a way of creating either a monologue or dialogue.

What about those of us who claim not to have an inner voice?

Strictly, this isn't true.

Everyone has an inner voice, but some of us are less aware of this voice, and with practice, we can learn to find our inner voice so that we can begin to make the right choices for ourselves.

Our inner monologue is what we hear, or what we tell ourselves. It serves as a reminder of what we need to do, or when we need to do things. Our inner monologue is important as it helps us to make mental checklists of the things we need to get done—our inner to-do list.

What we need to focus on for personal growth and development is our inner dialogue and our ability to have meaningful conversations with ourselves so that we can begin to encourage positive movement in our lives.

Most of us have several internal interlocutors, but the five most common ones are:

- The faithful friend: Personal strength, positive feeling, strong relationships.

- The ambivalent parent: Strength, self-love, positive criticism and feedback.
- The proud rival: Success-driven, healthy competition, creativity, problem-solving.
- The calm optimist: Positivity, gentle confidence.
- The helpless child: Lack of control, negative emotions, poor self-regulation.

In different situations, and with different mindsets, we will adopt these different roles within ourselves to help, or hinder, ourselves in different situations.

Our inner voice, and indeed, the type of internal interlocutor we choose to engage with, plays a massive role in our behaviors, our ability to problem-solve, in our critical thinking, and in our ability to self-regulate (Puchalska-Wasyl, 2014).

### Our Inner Voice: What Roles Does It Play?

Our inner voice, when used in the form of a dialogue, helps us to make decisions in our lives.

A good way to think of our inner voice is as an internal guidance system, or GPS.

If you have ever used a GPS in real life, you will know that sometimes it works really well, and other times it can get you more lost than if you tried to navigate an area yourself.

Most of the time, the GPS will get you frustratingly lost in an area that is totally foreign to you, or it may take you on some wildly inappropriate detour with the presumption that you would rather drive more distance than sit in traffic.

Either way, the GPS is designed to have us reach our final destination and will lead us on a journey with an end goal in mind.

Our inner voice, like the GPS, can play a positive or negative role in our lives, but both of these roles will get us to our destination, whether we want to or not.

On the positive side, our inner voice can give us a sense of belonging, help us live a happier, more fulfilled life, help us achieve success, allow us to cope with stress, build our confidence, and improve our cognitive abilities.

Conversely, when our inner voice is negative, we can create an internal crisis for ourselves through self-doubt, insomnia, feelings of hopelessness, and, ultimately, self-induced depression.

The beauty of our internal voice is that we are not a silent audience, listening in with no ability to provide input into the dialogue that is being had, and we all have the ability to guide our internal dialogue to one that facilitates positive growth.

In other words, you are in the driver's seat and you can choose to pull over and reprogram your GPS whenever you want to.

To re-program your GPS, you need to talk to your other internal voices so you can understand your inner critic and help it make the right decisions for you.

Remember, your inner critic is not all bad and certainly does serve a purpose when called upon. The trick is to learn when to listen to this helpless child and when to encourage it to set aside its fears so that you can grow.

## STEPS FOR PLACATING YOUR INNER HELPLESS CHILD

Every single one of us has two voices inside of us—the nurturing, positive, uplifting voice that tells us we can do anything we put our minds to, and the critical, discouraging voice that sabotages our positive growth in life.

The critical inner voice is not the one that tells you to take a moment before you act, or tries to instill reason in a moment, it is the nagging, whiny, persistent bully in the corner of our minds that tells us we're not capable of great things.

It's the voice that reminds you of your previous mistakes and failures and makes you believe that you're actually just not good enough for just about anything outside of your strengths.

Our inner critic never motivates us, and it certainly doesn't care if we grow, because growth is uncomfortable and requires us to set our egos aside.

This inner critic can be quieted, though, if you learn to listen to the voice of self-compassion, encouragement, and wide-eyed curiosity.

With the techniques I'll list below, you can not only become aware of your inner critic, but also find ways to talk to it and convince it to shut up. You can do this by bringing in your other natural interlocutors to help calm and quiet that critical voice.

### Meditation

Carl Jung once said, "Until you make the unconscious conscious, it will direct your life and you will call it fate" (C.G. Jung, n.d.).

You need to be aware of your inner critic and know what it is saying before you can change your inner dialogue, and meditation is a great way to bring your unconscious thought patterns into your consciousness.

Through meditation, we can recognize our thoughts, observe them, and then act on changing the way we think rather than just allowing these thoughts to rule our lives.

Always remember that our thoughts are merely based on our perceptions, and perceptions are not facts all of the time.

### Put a Face to the Voice

A great, and often hilarious, way to silence our inner critic is to put a face to the voice.

Consider the most amusing character you've ever seen on television or in a film, and match the face to the voice.

This technique may sound ridiculous, but it is incredibly powerful because it is very difficult to take anything seriously when we're laughing at its ridiculousness.

Choosing a character you deem to be funny will help you to diminish what they are saying, blowing it off as a joke rather than listening up and taking what the inner critic is saying to heart.

### Stop the Comparison Game

You are so incredibly unique that it is a damned shame to compare yourself to anyone else.

Competition is great. It helps to keep us motivated and pushes us to move forward in our lives, but we are all walking our own paths, living our own lives, and have our own strengths and weaknesses.

Self-criticism turns competition into a toxic internal game where we believe that we are not successful if we are not exactly like someone else.

Stop the comparison game and embrace who you are. Look inward, not outward, for the motivation to succeed, and soon enough, the realization will dawn on you that you are powerful beyond all measure if you allow yourself to be.

Besides, copies of an original are very rarely as great and definitely aren't as valuable.

### Be Self-Compassionate

It's time to accept that everything in life is imperfect.

Don't believe me?

Put your face through one of those symmetry mobile apps and see how strange you would look if your face were perfect.

Imperfection creates beauty and character, and without mistakes, some of the greatest inventions and, indeed, people of our times would never have come to be.

Everything from Post-Its to Penicillin and even those chocolate chip cookies we drown our sorrows in came to be because of something else failing and mistakes being made.

Life is not meant to be perfect, and self-compassion helps us to see that our mistakes and failures are actually wonderful opportunities presented to us.

### Daily Gratitude

The conscious practice of gratitude allows us to become aware of all of the great things that are happening in our lives. It is not about forcing ourselves to be positive all of the time or ignoring the issues we are facing.

Rather, it's the practice of acknowledging that bad days and bad situations will happen from time to time and that nothing is permanent if we change our mindset to what we are facing.

Daily self-gratitude allows us not only to reflect on the good things in our life but also on our own ability to overcome hard things, and when we can see how capable we are of it, it makes it easy to take on other hard tasks.

You need to be able to reason with, and then silence, your inner critic so that you can allow the other, more positive voices in your head to come through loudly, encouraging and motivating you toward success.

You simply cannot build success on a foundation of self-loathing and fear, and you need to build your inner confidence so that you have the wherewithal to come out on top as a high achiever.

## BUILDING YOUR INNER CONFIDENCE

If your inner critic is loudly professing that you cannot shed yourself from your old ways right now, allow me to be your cheerleader—you've got this! Now is the time to own your life!

Building your inner confidence will be one of the greatest gifts you ever give yourself, and the best thing about creating a confident version of yourself is that the entire process is in your control.

Let's take a look at some of the ways you can learn to become the confident person you're destined to be.

### Practice the Positive

Being positive is absolutely not being naive. You can still weigh up the pros and cons of your decisions, but at some point, you need to prepare, cross your fingers, and leap into the unknown.

Positivity and hope are a combination of preparation and faith in your abilities, and everyone is capable of both of these things.

Practicing positivity is purely the ability to believe that the hard work you have put into anything is enough to see you through to a positive outcome. And, when you're optimistic, it becomes far easier to brush yourself off when something goes wrong, because you know that you're properly prepared for the inevitable obstacles you'll face.

### Embrace Your Personal Power

Personal power is not about using your talents to manipulate others for your own good or benefit, it's about realizing that you have a natural state of power within so that it can help you to achieve your goals.

When you acknowledge your inner personal power, you can begin to harness the motivating energy and confidence you will require to achieve your goals and to make a positive difference in your life.

### Speak Up!

The perfectionist is a master of handing responsibility to others, and using phrases like, "Whatever you think is best," or "I don't know, you decide," are just cop-outs so that we don't have to take responsibility for a bad decision made.

Learn to speak up and make your opinions known. Make decisions and stick to those decisions, enjoying responsibility and accountability for where those decisions lead you.

I am by no means saying you should never compromise, but learn to accept responsibility for your thought processes and for your choices. Set fear aside and actually commit with conviction to your opinions and your choices.

### Frank Sinatra Your Life

He did it his way, and you can do it your way!

Your idiosyncrasies, weaknesses, and strengths make you incredible, and you have to live your way.

Yes, there will be times when you will need to conform, but conforming doesn't mean you cannot be unique either.

Learn to accept who you are, embrace it, and tackle those goals in a way that is as unique as you are.

The world doesn't need a dulled version of you; it needs you in full, glorious force, so ditch the mask, send fear packing, and let your inner confidence take hold of your future.

### Ignore the Haters

That includes your inner hater!

People are going to be envious of you, dislike you, and disagree with your ways, and that is fine—really it is.

We simply cannot accept that everyone needs to be the same thing, and when you can accept that you will have as many haters as you will cheerleaders, life becomes so much simpler.

You absolutely cannot please all of the people all of the time because everyone is different, and you need to take on the attitude of a young child—indifference to the opinions of others.

Remember, a person's decision to hate on you has nothing to do with you and everything to do with them and their insecurities.

Ignore the haters. You find pity, amusement, or even empathy in their efforts to derail you. After all, anyone's efforts to derail you are actually a compliment.

## YOUR INNER CONFIDENCE: DAILY EXERCISES

Your positive inner voice can be as loud and as prominent as your inner critic, and expressing this inner voice will help you to learn, grow, and nurture the wonderful person you are.

Tapping into your inner confidence allows you to take on your goals, conquer your fears, and understand what your purpose is.

The activities below are designed to be done every single day and will help you to strengthen your inner voice so that you can hear what it has to say and move toward achieving your dreams.

### *Guided Meditation to Strengthen Your Inner Voice*

The guided meditation below is taken directly from 3HO and is designed to help you strengthen your inner voice (*Meditation for Guidance: Strengthen the Inner Voice*, n.d.).

### Meditation for Guidance: Strengthen the Inner Voice

Time: 12–32 minutes

Number of exercises: 1

Intensity: low

This guided meditation helps you to harness the power of mantra repetition. When you confirm and reaffirm that you can hear yourself and what you are saying, you can begin to become more in tune with your own inner voice.

This meditation is meant to stop your inner critic from sowing seeds of doubt and frustration in your life.

**Part One**

Posture: Sit with a straight spine in Easy Pose or Lotus Pose.

Breath Pattern: Cup the hands lightly together. Leave a slit between the outer sides of the little fingers. Bow the head forward over the palms. Look into the palms, eyes barely open. Inhale in 10 short, sharp breaths, mentally saying the word, "Whaa-Ho" with each sharp breath.

Exhale out 10 short breaths, this time mentally saying "Guroo."

Continue for 11 minutes.

Then inhale powerfully, exhale powerfully, and relax.

**Part Two**

Posture and Mantra: Still sitting in Lotus Pose, bring your hands together as if you were praying.

Chant in a continuous monotone:

Whaa-Ho Whaa-Ho Whaa-Ho Whaa-Ho
Whaa-Ho Whaa-Ho Whaa-Ho Whaa-Ho
Guroo Guroo Guroo Guroo
Guroo Guroo Guroo Guroo

Continue for 5–11 minutes.

You may work up to 31 minutes.

### *Deep Listening Exercise*

Communication has two parts: Listening and speaking. When we "deep listen," we listen with the intent to hear what is being expressed by our inner voice.

To do this, you will need to find a quiet space to sit in reflection for 5 to 10 minutes.

When you are ready

- take a deep breath and begin to listen to your inner voice.
- ask yourself what that voice is trying to communicate to you.
- is the voice saying positive things or negative things?
- notice if you are conversing back with the voice.
- are you agreeing or disagreeing with what is being said?
- take a breath.

- stay grounded and challenge any negative thoughts.
- don't judge the process, simply observe your thoughts, accept them, challenge them, and let them go.

Your inner voice will help you to build the confidence you need to let go of your perfectionistic ways and will help you to move forward with your life and your goals.

The issue with being a perfectionist is that our intentions are good. We want to succeed, but far too often we get caught in the spiral of analyzing the outcome of our decisions over and over again.

We need to learn to commit and free ourselves from the spiral of analysis paralysis so that we can finally move forward toward success.

# 4

# THE SPIRAL OF THE ANALYSIS PARALYSIS

Analysis paralysis is a productivity killer that isn't spoken about nearly enough.

The perfectionist, in particular, believes that the more information they have about what they are doing, the better it will be and the easier it will be for them to make a decision.

Realistically speaking, if we are afraid to commit, no amount of information will ever be enough because we just don't want to have to make a decision in the first place.

## ANALYSIS PARALYSIS: AN OVERVIEW

Analysis paralysis happens to everyone once in a while, and it's entirely understandable because we live in a world that really does seem to offer us endless choices.

We'll open an online store, start browsing, and then stall or stop.

Most of the time, we think we know what we want to find, but somehow, we get caught up in comparing every single detail of the choices offered to us until we decide we can't decide what is best for us and we abandon the items in our cart.

And it isn't only online purchases that have us stuck in an endless loop of information either. Just about every area of our lives can be bogged down with entirely too much data, and the choice to move forward when confronted with all of these things in play, and in our minds, can feel impossible.

### *What Analysis Paralysis Looks Like*

Analysis paralysis doesn't happen all of the time, and there will be decisions we make that will not make us feel confused or overwhelmed. Most of the time, these easier-to-make decisions are the ones that we're used to making or that fall in line with what we deem to be our strengths.

Certain decisions, though, can leave us feeling like there's just too much going on and too much to consider, and we begin to spiral quickly into analysis paralysis.

Analysis paralysis can happen to just about everyone, especially when considering larger-life decisions like

- career
- starting a family, including adding a pet
- relationships and marriage
- finances

Experiencing analysis paralysis in these areas of our lives is totally normal. They are, after all, big decisions that can alter our own future and the future of others. We instinctively understand the gravity of these decisions we need to make, and it can weigh down on us heavily, causing us to overthink or seek the opinions of too many different sources or people.

Perfectionism, however, has us stuck in analysis paralysis for just about any decision we need to make, from what spread to put on our bread to whether or not we should be eating bread in the first place, and our attempts to make sense or find clarity in the decisions we make can consume us, leaving us feeling outright confused and overwhelmed.

### What Analysis Paralysis Feels Like

Above everything else, becoming paralyzed because of our choices increases our stress, but because we are all unique, this stress can feel different to different people.

Symptoms of stress usually make us feel overwhelmed and tired because of all the other bad feelings that are going on underneath.

These feelings include

- thoughts that we ruminate on endlessly, and which rob us of our time and our joy.
- feeling like, or actually having a heart rate that is unpleasantly rapid.
- panic attacks and persistent anxiety regardless of what we are doing.
- shallow breathing as a result of increased anxiety and panic.
- insomnia, nightmares, and broken sleep that only compounds our fatigue.
- abandoning decision making altogether because it's just too hard.
- lack of productivity because we are stuck in our thoughts and decision-making process.
- an inability to focus on anything other than the information pertaining to the decision at hand.

Stress is a killer, literally and figuratively, and freeing ourselves from it, as well as learning how to manage it correctly, is imperative to living a healthy, happy life. But perfectionism, and certainly analysis paralysis, robs us of our ability to live a manageably stressed life.

*Analysis Paralysis Traits*

Some things make our normal analysis paralysis worse, and once we look at these things, it's easier to see why perfectionists can get stuck in a state of analysis paralysis that never goes away.

## Black and White Thinking

When we think in terms of everything being either good or bad for us, or have an all-or-nothing attitude, we can become stuck in the decision-making process. This is because the world is full of color, and even if we insist on staying in our black and white ways, there are a whole lot of shades of those too—have you ever tried to wear an all-black ensemble?

It's frustrating enough to try and find the right shades of black that match perfectly, let alone be told that we need to embrace all of the colors of the rainbow, and then some, and so it becomes difficult to decide which decisions fit into one category or another.

To be a good decision-maker and a high achiever in general, you need to develop both emotional and cognitive flexibility. This means that you need to get rid of your rigid way of thinking.

Perfectionists are, by nature, extremely cautious people. We don't like the outside world or any of its colors to pervade our safe space because it overwhelms us and makes us fearful.

The fact is that the world is full of unknowns and the potential outcomes of our actions are almost limitless, especially when we do not commit at all.

There is no way for us to predict an outcome—wouldn't life be easier if we could—and sometimes we need to commit to the actions we will need to take for the best possible outcome, accepting whatever positive end result happens for us.

### Trying to People Please

In case you haven't quite understood this yet, you cannot please everyone all of the time. It's as impossible as trying to be perfect, and when you try to make people happy, it comes with a cost—your own happiness.

Making decisions that may or may not definitely impact others is tough. To be honest, it outright stinks, but it is part of being a functioning adult, and when we can weigh in with the people who matter, taking their opinion into account, it becomes slightly easier to decide what the best thing is for everyone.

### Low or No Confidence

Let's face it, you need to have pretty large kahunas to get up every single day and chase your dreams, especially when chasing your dreams means making on-the-spot decisions that could potentially catapult your success forward and bring you to a grinding stop.

Having confidence doesn't change the outcome of these decisions, but it does allow you to be at peace with the consequences of your choices, and that makes all the difference when dealing with life's many obstacles.

Experiencing analysis paralysis is uncomfortable and plain overwhelming, and when we take a step back to properly rationalize the condition, it is actually far more painful than making a decision and following through with it.

Procrastination is one of the symptoms of perfectionism, and because perfectionists fear being able to complete a task perfectly, they often put it off as long as possible.

As you now know, this primarily stems from fear of not meeting the goal set out exactly, or that something bad or wrong will thrust the perfectionist into the spotlight, stripping them bare so that everyone can examine their flaws.

The more a perfectionist fears failure or ridicule, the more likely they are to procrastinate. A Low tolerance for frustration can mean the perfectionist enters into a downward spiral of self-loathing and confirmation that they are the failures they thought they were.

I want to be clear here, procrastination is by no means laziness. It is a misguided sense that we are getting things done when actually we aren't.

When we perceive a challenge or goal to be outside of our realms of comfort, we fear it because there is a greater chance of making a mistake or failing, and so we sidestep this discomfort by diverting our attention to all of the things we 'need' to do to appear perfect.

Delaying tasks leads us to one outcome—the thought process takes longer than the task itself, and while we know that procrastination is an easy spot, we still get caught up in it.

An easy way to know whether you're procrastinating is to ask yourself, "Am I doing the things I need to be doing, or am I doing other things like thinking about the task at hand?" If you answered yes to the latter of these two questions, you're procrastinating, and it's up to you to determine why exactly that is.

Some of the more common reasons we procrastinate are

- task difficulty
- task anxiety
- fear of imperfection
- lack of self-confidence
- confusion in priorities
- lack of focus
- boredom
- indecision

If you don't know what to do, how to do it, and you're not enjoying doing it, you're going to procrastinate. It's really that simple.

So how do we overcome analysis paralysis once and for all?

### Overcoming Analysis Paralysis

Ruminating thoughts, slow progress, or no progress at all can make it difficult to avoid procrastination.

Finding ourselves in a state of analysis paralysis is overwhelming, and sometimes we just don't know how to escape the clutches of the condition.

The steps laid out below will help you to free yourself from the grip of analysis paralysis and will clear the fog of confusion you are experiencing so that you can develop a sense of confidence in your decision-making processes.

### You Have to Recognize It

The first step to getting out of any state of being is to first realize you are actually in it. Take the time to sit quietly and scan your body, recognizing any tension you may be carrying, and allowing yourself to observe your thoughts.

Are these thoughts ruminating?

What are they saying?

Allow yourself to look at what is happening from an outsider's point of view so that you can take the necessary steps to free yourself.

## Allow for Flexibility

You cannot break free from analysis paralysis if you persist in people-pleasing, fear, rigid thought processes, and right-speaking.

You will have to remind yourself, often, that it is okay to be imperfect and flexible in your thought processes.

Remember that your fear of being imperfect is holding you back and definitely not serving your purpose.

## Believe in Your Capabilities

It's natural to be fearful of an outcome, but you need to understand that you can recover from just about anything if you commit to the steps required to fix your mistakes.

What is critical to remember is that fear and excitement often feel the same, and being uncomfortable or fearful may just be your intuition telling you that something exciting is about to happen to you.

## Stop Valuing Other Opinions Over Your Own

The opinion of others can be valuable, but what others think should really have no value in your life and your choices, especially if those choices do not affect these other people.

You need to learn to make an intentional choice to stop asking other people for their input into your life, especially when all of the information you need is inside of you already.

**Stop Predicting the Future**

When we're paralyzed by everything we think could happen, we look into the future more than we should, trying to anticipate the outcome of our choices. This is unhealthy and actually won't help us to avoid anything negative that is going to happen in any case.

It's great to be prepared, but making smaller, more immediate choices to help facilitate our goals is far more important than looking to the future constantly.

## TASKS TO OVERCOME ANALYSIS PARALYSIS

Few exercises are as useful or as effective as mindfulness and becoming aware of your thoughts and how your ruminating thoughts particularly hinder your progress in life.

Mindfulness teaches us to be tolerant and to accept that our thoughts have enormous power over us, or none at all if we choose for them not to.

### *Exercise in Mindfulness*

There are a couple of different ways we can practice mindfulness. I have outlined the basics of how mindfulness works and how you can practice it daily. Please feel free to research other methods so that you can find one that works well for you.

1. Learn to pay attention. I know that it is hard to slow down and notice things, especially when you are caught up in your thoughts, but take the time to stop and take in your environment and the wonderful things that surround you.
2. Learn to live in the moment, being intentional in your ability to accept that life happens and that you can concentrate on the things that matter to you.
3. Learn to accept yourself and treat yourself in the same way you would treat your best friend.
4. Learn to breathe. Breathing exercises can help you to pull yourself out of anxiety quickly and effectively.

Other forms of mindfulness include body scanning, sitting meditation, and walking meditation. Find whatever works for you and practice it as often as you need to until you pull yourself out of analysis paralysis.

### The Analytic Paralysis Checklist

If you are finding it difficult to make a decision, and if you have identified that you are in a state of paralysis, use the checklist below to help you pull yourself out of it.

| Checklist Item | Yes | No |
|---|---|---|
| I will jump in even if I am not sure–fake it until you make it | | |
| I will be positive–inner confidence | | |
| I will challenge my inner critic–silence the helpless child | | |
| I will practice patience–self-compassion and empathy | | |
| I will create personal boundaries–work within purpose | | |
| I will be true to myself–value own opinion | | |
| I will internally validate–negate external validation | | |
| I will act confident even if I am not–smile, shoulders back, superhero pose | | |

## *Exercise in Acceptance*

Sometimes we need to just accept that our lives are what they are because we made a couple of bad choices, but you are still here, still breathing, and still have the power to change your circumstances.

Learning acceptance can help us to free ourselves of the past and give us an opportunity to move forward to a life of success.

## Step 1: Witness Your Own Judgment

When we struggle to accept anything in our life, it usually stems from our inner judgment and bias. You will need to observe how and why you are judging yourself so that you can learn to come to peace with your past mistakes.

## Step 2: Start a List of Positives

Use the sheet provided below and in the main column, write whatever it is that you are battling to accept.

In the adjacent column, write all of the positive things that may come from these situations.

For example, I am battling to accept I lost my job—I have the opportunity to get back into the workforce, doing something I love. I have learned from my previous experience that perfectionism slowed my productivity and hindered my team's performance.

Focus on the situation at hand and write everything down, even if it feels insignificant.

## Step 3: Check in With Your Emotions

Reread your list and focus on how you are feeling. Are these emotions positive or negative?

If you are still feeling negative, you will need to stop and enter into a few moments of mindfulness so that you can let go of your feelings and move forward into a more positive frame of thought.

| I am struggling with; | The positives of this situation are; |
| --- | --- |
| | |
| | |
| | |
| | |
| | |
| | |
| | |
| | |
| | |

As a perfectionist, we get caught in analysis paralysis often, mostly because we fear imperfection and failure, but the reality is that we need to fail before we succeed.

We need to learn to accept this failure so that we can begin to embrace it for the amazing opportunity it actually is.

5

# TO SUCCEED YOU MUST FAIL

*Failure is constructive feedback that tells you to try a different approach to accomplish what you want.*

— IDOWU KOYENIKAN

If I had a dime for the number of times people have told me they wish they knew what success meant, they would be rich. I would be... Well, not rich because the value of money changes in the same way that success does.

Success and our personal success stories differ, but with two common characteristics:

1. It is never too late to begin your journey to success.

2. You are the master of your own success and what success means to you.

Just like different things, like our titles, money, social status, family, etc., can motivate us, they are also the labels we assign to what success means to us.

For some of us, we don't feel that we are successful if we don't achieve greatness in these labels, and it leaves us feeling lost and wondering what exactly success is.

The issue with driving our success based on these labels is that we have not defined what success means to us, and that is an issue because we cannot work with a sense of purpose toward what really matters to us.

Success varies, not just in how successful we are, but in what we are successful in. For example, you may want to be successful in raising your children to be happy, healthy, and well-adjusted adults.

The definition of success is not just something that you need to define for yourself, but ultimately, when working within your purpose, it defines you.

There is no one-size-fits-all approach to success, and how you define success or achieve it is entirely up to you.

Understanding what success means to you doesn't just happen overnight, especially when you have spent a large part of your life people-pleasing and chasing perfection.

You're going to need to dig deep and find the courage to ask yourself some pretty tough questions to uncover the heart of your own success journey.

## WHY WE'RE AFRAID TO FAIL

Failure isn't happening or being done, according to the dictionary. More specifically, failure is: a) not doing a duty or expected action; b) being unable to do a normal function; c) a sudden stop of normal functioning; or d) breaking or giving way under stress (Definition of Failure, Marriam Webster Dictionary, n.d.).

Looking at these definitions, it becomes easy to see why we are afraid of failure, but these descriptions also tell us a couple of things:

1. That failure can happen to anything or anyone.
2. That failure depends on success first.

Fearing failure, therefore, is actually fearing success, and the fear of failure may affect us differently. Fear of failure or success can be hard to spot because we try to hide it by making other excuses for not following through so we don't have to face how we feel.

Let me be clear, fear is scary!

No one goes through life wanting to face the monster under their bed. We have to go through crippling thoughts, agonizing anxiety, and sleepless nights before we decide to grab a flashlight and shine it in the dark places under our beds.

Likewise, fearing failure and success comes about for a number of reasons:

- We don't believe we have the knowledge, insight, or skill required to achieve.
- We feel like our goals are unachievable because they are not clearly defined or outside of our purpose.
- We procrastinate and get caught up in our analysis paralysis for so long that our ability to achieve our goal is severely hindered due to time constraints.
- We focus on our shortcomings, weaknesses, and the blooper reels of our lives.
- We fret about whether people will judge us for our shortcomings,
- We are worried that we will disappoint others because of our failures.

### How a Fear of Failure Brings Success to a Screeching Halt

Without plunging you deeply into a chapter of Freudian psychology, developing a fear of failure happens over time and can usually be traced back to critical elements that were lacking in your upbringing, trauma experienced, a deep lack of self-esteem, or a fragile ego.

Regardless of what the cause of your fear of failure is, being stuck in that fear can take a heavy toll on your mental and physical health and can shake your beliefs to the core as you wrestle with trying to find the motivation to succeed while beating off fear, doubt, and self-disapproval.

The impacts of a fear of failure include

- a low self-esteem–critical and negative self-talk.
- a low or no motivation to get started–analysis paralysis.
- a chronic case of self-sabotage–finding reasons to self-handicap and undermine efforts.
- a deep feeling of shame–self-predicting failure as a result of fearful behaviors.

I am not denying that failure hinders growth, but this hindrance is temporary if we do not allow the fear of failure to overtake our ability to learn from our failures.

Failure is not only important to success, but it is also the cornerstone of achievement, and when we know why failure is so critical, we can reach for that flashlight, dispelling our fears of a perceived monster under our bed, or in our head in this case.

## WHY FAILURE IS IMPORTANT FOR SUCCESS

As a professional athlete, you are taught that you will fail a lot before you succeed.

You will fail almost 70% of the time, and as long as you are within the 30% success rate, you are seen to be an incredibly high-achieving professional.

Failure is not the end of the world, it actually opens you up to a world of opportunity, and when you can set aside negative self-talk and feelings of shame, failure can be your greatest ally in achieving success.

Failure offers up a unique opportunity to grow, but only if you choose to learn from the things you did wrong. It's okay to make mistakes—heck, it's even human—but unless we examine these mistakes and choose to change where we go wrong, they are only the reason for your failure.

You need to be conscious in choosing how you respond to your failure, because through conscious thought comes inspired change.

When you fail, we open up new opportunities for you, and believe me when I say, sometimes when you screw up the first path entirely and you're totally lost, the right path opens up for you. Life is about figuring out what you truly enjoy doing and then pursuing those things with passion. Remember that failure is merely a path to success, not a set course.

Ultimately, when you fail, you are given an amazing opportunity to evaluate your strong and weak points so that you can improve upon both.

Success requires you to evaluate, and then reevaluate the steps you have taken to get to where you are now, and when it comes down to it, failure allows you to make a choice—to get back up and make yourself stronger or to stay down. And really, failure isn't true failure unless you choose to not get back up.

### The Link Between Failure and Success

I'd like you to take a moment to ask yourself a question.

Reflect on this question before you continue with this chapter so that what you read really resonates with you.

The question is: Are you truly failing, or are you failing to learn?

We all have our own personal failures and successes. Some of these successes may have been minor, or they could have been great, and I guarantee that at least one of these failures sucked and threatened to make us throw in the towel.

Success of any kind requires us to be patient, not just with our processes but with the lessons we need to learn from our failures.

And here's the thing, mistakes aren't failures. Not achieving what we set out to achieve is not a failure. Thinking about giving up is not failure, because every mistake and every missed attempt at success is an opportunity to gain insight into where we need to learn and grow.

Thomas Edison once said, "I have not failed, I've found 10,000 ways that won't work" (Edison, n.d). This statement is a powerful testament to the fact that being successful requires you to be resilient while you learn what doesn't work.

Trust me when I say there is no right or wrong way to achieve our goals, unscrupulous and devious behavior aside, and we will never succeed at anything in life if we choose to stop learning from the mistakes we have made.

"Failing fast" is a phrase from Silicon Valley that means looking for failure on purpose so that weaknesses can be found and fixed faster. The goal is to get to success faster.

Deliberately making mistakes, or failing even, helps you to achieve what you need to achieve quicker, but only if you choose to see failure for what it actually is.

There are so many reasons why failure and success are inter-linked, but at the center of all of these reasons is that you learn from what went right and what went wrong.

Mistakes require that you believe in yourself and have enough courage to turn inward—assess and address your weaknesses, flaws, and mistakes.

Failure leads to success because:

- It allows you the opportunity to grow as a person, pushing you outside of your comfort zone into great things.
- It provides you with the opportunity to increase your confidence in your ability to do hard things.
- It allows you to handle stress better, teaching you that stress and excitement are basically the same things if you reframe your perceptions.
- It gives you a chance to see how brave you really are as you step into the unknown.
- It teaches you that few skills in life are equal to resilience.
- It teaches you that patience and compassion for others and yourself are more valuable than being perfect.
- It shows you that success is a journey to be enjoyed and that often the blooper reel is far more entertaining than the main show.

Failure isn't failure until we have given up. When we choose not to overcome an obstacle, or decide that we would rather be stuck in our discomfort than to slowly pull ourselves out of the perfectionist trap, we are failing. Everything else is just a mistake that can be corrected along the way.

## THE ACTIONABLE STEPS FOR CONTINUING AFTER FAILURE

It's perfectly normal to go through phases in your life where your confidence drops suddenly, especially when you feel like your endeavors have amounted to nothing.

Lacking confidence is counterproductive, though, as it forces you to waste precious time second-guessing and sometimes feeling sorry for yourself.

Regaining your confidence is a must, not only for you to become successful, but so that you can end the pity party for one that you are throwing, and get on with the business of achieving.

The exercises below are designed to help you regain your confidence, forgive your past mistakes, and overcome your fear of failure.

### *Confidence Building Exercise*

Building your confidence will help you see your mistakes as great chances to learn, help you become more resilient, and give you the 'chutzpah' you need to be a very successful person.

### Strategy 1: Stop Focusing on the Mistake

Success requires you to take a look at what went right and what went wrong, but dwelling on all of the wrongness is just going to knock your confidence around.

The easiest way to stop focusing on your mistakes is to write down what went wrong and then beef up your weaknesses or skills in the areas that created an issue for you.

While this sounds overly simplistic, it actually works in two ways—it removes your focus from the negative and builds confidence through a new skill learned.

Ask yourself,

- What could I have done differently?
- What lessons can be learned from this false start?
- How will I upskill myself so that the same mistakes won't be made?

It's important to focus on what can be done rather than beating yourself up over what was done.

**Strategy 2: Forgive Yourself**

Forgiving anyone, including yourself, allows you to move forward and try to fix what went wrong.

The exercise below will help you go through the steps of how to practice self-empathy and forgiveness.

Forgiveness isn't as easy as saying sorry and moving on, though, and you will need to first be honest with yourself about what has happened when making your mistakes and why they happened.

**Strategy 3: Shut That Inner Critic Up**

The only way you're ever going to get the nagging voice in your head to shut up is to challenge it.

Personal dialogues are important because they build you up or break you down in some cases, and it's your responsibility to silence the negativity in your mind. This is easier said than done, though, because sometimes it can feel like we're shifting blame and responsibility for mistakes happening.

To truly keep your inner critic at bay and to continue to accept responsibility, you need to learn to paraphrase what is happening in your head. For example, instead of saying, "I achieved absolutely nothing and I really screwed this up. I can't do anything right!" Rather say, "Well, I didn't perform well on this task. Let's explore where I went wrong so that I can fix these mistakes. I am capable if I know all of the facts!"

Negative self-talk only ever sets you back from achieving success, and because your brain is pre-wired to think negatively (thanks to evolution), it is really easy for your inner critic to throw all other inner voices off of center stage to hog the limelight.

**Strategy 4: Provide Context to Failure**

By putting your situation into perspective, you'll see that, first and foremost, you haven't failed yet, and second, you are not the sum of all your failures.

You are a person, and you cannot be defined by an outcome, only by your behavior. When you provide context to the situation, you are showing yourself that you are not a failure and that you are meant to experience mistakes in order for you to learn.

## Strategy 5: Assess Whether Past Mistakes Have Led to Success

You will need to consistently remind yourself that you have made mistakes in the past and have thrived despite making these mistakes.

Self-reflection is a powerful tool in reminding ourselves that our identity and our learning processes are two totally separate things.

If you cannot remember a time when you made a mistake and thrived anyway, do yourself a favor, pick a point in the room you're in, walk to that point, and then walk back. Or, make yourself a cup of coffee, continue to read this book, brush your teeth, tie your shoes, make your bed... You get the picture. All of these things didn't come easily to you. You tried, you failed, you tried again, you failed again, until eventually you got it right.

Success is the same process—you need to keep trying!

## Step 6: Attempt, Retry, and Repeat

Which leads us to the final step—you need to keep trying.

Rome wasn't built in a day and neither will you be. If you stop trying, then you have failed and you will have proved your inner critic's point.

You are designed to fail so that you can get up and try again until you get it right. Trial and error will always teach you the most important lessons, so make the most of it.

### Overcoming Your Fear of Failure

Take a look at the table below. Using the areas provided to you, you can learn how to rationalize your fear of failure and overcome it.

Remember to be thoughtful and intentional in your answers.

This exercise can be done as many times as you like to help you overcome your fear of failure once and for all.

Complete the failure-based sentences typed for you below:

| | |
|---|---|
| **My thoughts on this failure are** | |
| | |
| | |
| **My feelings on this failure are** | |
| | |
| | |
| **The actions that led to this failure are** | |
| | |
| | |
| **What behaviors led to this failure** | |
| | |
| | |
| **What lessons have I learned** | |
| | |
| | |
| **How can I redefine this failure** | |
| | |
| | |
| **What have I done to boost my confidence** | |
| | |
| | |
| **I have forgiven my failure by** | |
| | |
| | |

## *A Practical Exercise in Self Forgiveness*

Self-forgiveness helps you to deal with your mistakes in a healthy way, allowing you to move forward and try again.

Judging yourself is a form of self-condemnation, and choosing to forgive yourself sets you free from the guilt and shame of the mistakes you have made.

Remember that self-forgiveness does not absolve you from responsibility, nor does it give you an excuse to repeat your past behaviors.

Now that you know why self-forgiveness is important, you can take the steps necessary to forgive yourself for your past mistakes.

1. Find a quiet spot and set aside between 5 and 10 minutes of uninterrupted time.
2. Focus on your breath, breathing in and out at a comfortable rhythm.
3. Once you have your breathing under control, start to listen to your thoughts. Do not judge any of these thoughts, just observe them as they pop into your head.
4. Now consciously acknowledge these judgments, before forgiving your mistakes.
5. Sit in silence for a little while longer—listening to your thoughts once more.
6. Hone in on any limiting beliefs you may be thinking.
7. Forgive these limiting beliefs first and then challenge them by replacing them with positive beliefs.
8. Sit in silence one last time.

9. Now, offer yourself love. Think of yourself as a small child who requires nurturing, support, and unconditional love. Then give all of these things to yourself.

Overcoming the paralysis that comes with perfectionism isn't easy, but by learning to manage your stress and changing your mindset, you can rid yourself of the unsettling pressure of perfectionism.

6

# THE UNSETTLING PRESSURE OF PERFECTIONISM

S tress is an absolute jerk, and after the last few years of uncertainty in world events, most of us have had our stress levels at an all-time high.

For some of us, stress manifests with external signs that we aren't doing too great, while others of us wither into a metaphorical ball slowly dying inside.

Regardless of what your particular brand of stress symptom is, sore muscles, sweaty palms, or an inner critic that refuses to be silenced, stress that isn't managed is a killer—it messes with productivity and physical health, and ruins lives as it agonizingly corrodes self-confidence.

Learning to deal with stress and the pressure that comes with being a high achiever is important because most of the time, when we're faced with stressful situations, we revert to our old, negative, bad habits.

Most of us believe that stress is controlled by our brains and that our thoughts are responsible for the levels of stress we feel, and while that is partially true, it is not the full picture.

Stress is, as a matter of fact, controlled by our nervous system, and our nervous system is responsible for that pesky fight or flight response we have that increases our heart rate, narrows our blood vessels, and gets us ready to take on whatever big bad our brain thinks is going to attack us. When our thoughts are negative all of the time, or we're constantly calling ourselves names and belittling ourselves, our nervous system responds in the same way it would if someone else were doing these things, and it prepares us to defend our honor, not knowing that we are going to fight ourselves. It's a scene reminiscent of the film *Fight Club*.

When it comes down to it, we all feel stress, but some of us manage it differently, and some of us know how to reframe stress, embracing it as a temporary gift that helps us get out of difficult situations.

## ARE HIGH PERFECTIONISTS ALWAYS STRESSED OUT?

The short answer to that question is 'yes,' but the reasons for this are quite complex and require a little more explanation.

High achievers and perfectionists are not that different when it comes to stress, but it's how stress manifests and how it is managed and dealt with that differs quite dramatically.

Stress can actually be a good thing. It can push us to achieve our goals and give us the strength to deal with any problems that come our way.

A variety of factors can contribute to stress in our lives, and the high achiever is not immune to stress, depression, or any of the other issues that everyone faces in life.

For the high achiever, unique stressors do definitely come into play, though, and these can include:

- imposter syndrome.
- a deep fear of losing everything.
- being lonely.
- guilt for their achievements.

Even the positive life changes a high achiever attains may have them feeling stressed out, and it's usually these positive changes that drive the high achiever to feel guilt, or that they will lose everything if they do not continue to achieve.

High achievers, however, have mastered ways to manage their stress, buffering their emotional energy reserves, understanding their limits, balancing their lives, developing resilience over time, and assuming multifaceted identities to help them transition from one task to the next.

Above all of these thoughts, the high achiever works in accordance with their purpose, and this means they are fueled more by passion than they are by stress.

### The Perfectionist's Stress

When perfectionists feel stress, it can be from any number of things happening externally or internally. For the perfectionist, most of this stress comes from our inner critic, and the pressure we place on ourselves to be perfect all of the time.

The table below is meant to help you figure out if you're stressed out all the time or not:

| How You Feel | How You React | How You Behave |
| --- | --- | --- |
| Anxious | Headaches | Withdraw |
| Scared | Nausea | Indecisive or inflexible |
| Angry or aggressive | Digestive issues | Snap |
| Sad | Difficulty breathing | Be tearful |
| Irritable | Sweaty | Have issues sleeping |
| Frustrated | Rapid heartbeat | Fidget and procrastinate |
| Depressed | Muscle aches and pains | Use substances |

When stress is chronic, or lasts a long time, sleep becomes disrupted, the memory becomes limited, and brain fog sets in. Some research even suggests that IBS, heart disease, and stomach ulcers can happen when we are under stress for too long (Yaribeygi et al., 2017).

While just about everyone can identify with one or more of these stress-related issues, some people, like perfectionists, are more affected by stress than others.

When both perfectionism and stress are left unchecked, it can make it difficult to get up in the morning, let alone find the strength or the motivation to get ourselves out of the front door so that we can face the world.

## WHAT PRESSURE TO EXPECT ON YOUR JOURNEY TO SUCCESS

Success is the ultimate goal we strive for, regardless of what our definition of success is, but the expectations that accompany success can often feel overwhelming, and for many of us, feeling the pressure of becoming successful is enough to create enormous amounts of stress.

A long time ago, I realized that it wasn't so much the expectation of success that was weighing me down in anxiety, it was the expectations I placed on myself that had me stressed out.

And look, dealing with pressure in life is just not optional, especially if we want to become successful. Even the most successful people in the world deal with pressure and the stress that accompanies it, but there is a reason that successful people don't crumble under the weight of stress— several reasons to be exact.

To be fair, it's a tough ask to rate how well you're going to manage stress and pressure on your journey to success without actually throwing you into the thick of things.

For successful people, there are three common types of stress. They're not the normal stress we everyday folk experience, but on your journey to success, you will almost definitely come into contact with one of these three.

1. Anticipatory stress: The stress we feel before doing what we have set out to do, regardless of how prepared we are. For example, taking a big exam, competing in a sporting event, launching a new business, etc.
2. Shock events: Situations that are totally outside of our control but that just happen for whatever reason. For example, accidents, medical emergencies, chronic illness, etc.
3. Slow burn stress: Unidentified chronic stress that isn't managed by a person.

The issue with stress and pressure is that it throws that anxiety switch we perfectionists have into overdrive, and this can fill our collective minds with unwanted, intrusive thoughts that can make it almost impossible to think clearly.

You need to be able to flip the switch back to calm, cool, and collected so that you can better equip yourself for the inevitable pressure and stress you will encounter.

Even if you're one of the not-so-lucky ones who have been born with a predisposition to anxiety and stress, you can train yourself to be cool and calm under pressure.

Of course, this takes time and effort, but it is worth it, especially when you can rise above the pressure to reap the huge rewards it has to offer.

If all of this sounds very scary to you, remember, there can be no diamond without pressure, and it's up to you to learn how to put this pressure to its best use rather than be crushed by it.

### Perfectionism, Pressure, and Stress

Being a perfectionist means feeling dissatisfied with what you have achieved all of the time. Small mistakes are seen as huge failures, and receiving constructive criticism or negative feedback is like taking a stake to the heart.

Perfectionists become weighted down by the fear of just never being good enough, and pride is something that just doesn't exist in the realms of perfectionists.

Rather than being motivated to achieve our goals, we see them as something that will reassert our failure, and our high expectations of ourselves mean that we feel like we are constantly falling short of what we set out to do.

It's hard to enjoy the path to success when you're always worried about how your actions will turn out or stuck in a loop of thinking about what you could do differently to get the best result.

Being a perfectionist, in a nutshell, is stressful!

We create situations in which we procrastinate until there's just not enough time to get a task done, and then we feel stressed out because we procrastinated, but we know that we have to get it done, so we complete the task—then we aren't happy about the result, and so we beat ourselves up some more over why we shouldn't have started sooner, and all the while, our inner critic verbally lashes us with all of the reasons we just aren't good enough!

Quite a mouthful, isn't it? But this is the loop we find ourselves in when we procrastinate in a perfectionist's world, and it's agonizing, especially since we are the cause of our own stress and we know it.

Perfectionism enhances and solidifies our negative thoughts. Our inner critic becomes sort of a self-fulfilling prophecy because we tell ourselves we can't do something and we procrastinate and stress to the point that we really cannot.

These negative thoughts fuel a deep fear of making mistakes and of being perceived as not good enough, and stress and anxiety become the order of the day. The issue with perfectionism is that it drives us to be perfect in an imperfect world, and that in itself is stressful.

Add the fact that most perfectionists are just not getting enough sleep because ruminating thoughts and inner critics have no downtime, and a recipe for stressed-out disaster is created.

Perfectionism sucks the joy out of life and it hinders us from experiencing life for what it should be—a fun, messy experience in which we learn and grow, and living in a perpetual state of stress does nothing to reassert that life is actually fun.

For perfectionists, burnout from stress is a real possibility, and when we step away from perfectionism, we must do so in a healthy way that allows us to manage our stress as well as our behaviors for success.

## THE WORLD OF BURNOUT

When our perfectionism overtakes our lives, it can lead to burnout.

Burnout is a state we enter into when we are completely, totally, and physically exhausted. It occurs when we are subjected to long periods of stress.

As you know, perfectionism is stressful, and as such, it can trigger burnout.

Burnout can happen to anyone, though, and it's important that you are able to differentiate between self-critical behaviors that can lead to burnout, as opposed to burnout that happens for other reasons like stressful life events.

Perfectionism burnout can feel like

- we're emotionally numb.
- we're constantly overwhelmed.
- daily tasks are just not worth our energy.
- we're underappreciated no matter what we do.
- we have no motivation to do anything.
- we're hopeless or helpless.
- we're tired all the time.

Perfectionism triggers burnout because of the enormous amounts of stress we place on ourselves throughout our life. We live in a cycle of stress that has little or no relief, and a constant sense of despair follows us around like a dark stormy cloud that threatens us.

When we're bogged down by neverending stress because of our standard of perfection, we open ourselves up to burnout, and ironically, burnout reinforces our negative thoughts that we can't achieve anything or that we are weak.

Because we are perfectionists, negative self-talk becomes even louder once we reach burnout and we ask ourselves what is wrong with us that we cannot do anything. The issue with burnout is that there is literally nothing left in you to fight off your stress response and your body and mind have gone from asking for a break to forcing the matter.

### *Avoiding Burnout*

You don't need to be a perfectionist to experience burnout. A lot of people go through situations in their lives that force their mind and body to hit the reset button, demanding we rest and recuperate from our stress.

There are ways to avoid burnout, and the most important of these is to learn to manage our perfectionist ways.

This can be done by:

- Reminding yourself that the world is an imperfect place and that you need to be realistic with your expectations of yourself and others.
- Gathering perspective and looking at the bigger picture rather than the minute details.
- Compromising on any unrealistic expectations you have set for yourself.
- Speaking up and setting boundaries for yourself so that you can unwind when you need to.
- Managing your time correctly so that you avoid procrastinating tasks.
- Taking regular breaks from set tasks by doing activities you enjoy.
- Learning to manage your breath and lower your anxiety levels.
- Getting regular exercise, preferably outdoors.
- Taking time to be mindful so that you can understand what is causing your stress.

- Creating a support structure you trust.
- Prioritizing your sleep.

Stress and pressure can be managed, but just like stress is unique, perfectionist stress requires you to take the right steps to help you avoid burnout and keep your stress to a minimum.

## BREATH FOCUS TO REDUCE STRESS

Breathing may be an automatic function of our bodies, but we do have some control over it.

When we are feeling stressed, our breathing goes a little haywire, and our breathing rates and patterns change to get us ready to defend ourselves.

Deliberately changing our own breathing helps us to manage our stress levels and bypass the fight or flight response by flooding our bodies with oxygen and temporarily distracting our brain from a perceived threat.

The two breathing exercises below are incredibly effective in not just reducing stress levels but also in shutting down our fight or flight response. When combined with mindfulness, these breathing exercises can help to clear our minds of ruminating thoughts and refocus them on what we want to think of.

### Lion's Breath

Also known as Lion's Pose or Simhasana, Lion's Breath is an energizing yoga pose that helps to refocus the body and mind.

## Directions

1. Get yourself into a comfortable seated position.
2. Place your palms on your knees, spreading your fingers apart widely.
3. Press your palms down so that there is a slight pressure on your knees.
4. When you are comfortable, inhale deeply through your nose. Make sure your eyes are open wide.
5. Now, open your mouth wide and stick your tongue out, directing the tip toward your chin.
6. Contract the muscles in your throat and exhale, making a 'ha' sound as you exhale.
7. Repeat 2 or 3 times.
8. You can change your pose to whatever feels most comfortable for you. There is no right or wrong way for you to learn this breathing technique.

### Pursed Lip Breathing

This breathing technique is simple to learn and effectively slows down our breathing, ensuring we are deliberately taking in deep, long breaths.

You can practice pursed-lip breathing at any time.

**Directions**

1. Find a comfortable position. You can sit, stand, or even lie down.
2. Draw your focus to your neck and shoulders, consciously releasing tension.
3. Keep your mouth closed, and begin to inhale slowly through your nose. Count to 3.
4. Now pucker your lips like you're about to whistle and begin to exhale slowly.
5. Exhale for a count of 6.
6. Repeat 5 times.

Managing your stress is a great place to start, especially knowing that being a high achiever will come with its own set of stress. Having said that, if we don't seek to manage all of the components that cause our stress, we are basically paddling upstream.

This leads us to our final perfectionistic side effect—anxiety.

# 7

# THE ANXIETY WHIRLWIND

nxiety can be crippling, and it can drive us to behaviors that may be uncharacteristic or that may feel safe in the moment.

Perfectionism and indecision are often a byproduct of anxiety, and when we temporarily lose our ability to regulate our emotions because we are experiencing anxiety, our perfectionist tendencies can tend to run amok.

The pressure to be unique, perfect, and wealthy in modern society is overwhelming. We are bombarded by altered images all over the internet, and it seems we cannot escape the unrealistic expectation of being all things at all times.

Celebrities like Ariana Grande, Lizzo, Kendall Jenner, Camila Cabello, and Miley Cyrus have all shared their battles with anxiety and how they manage the symptoms of the condition.

## WHAT IS ANXIETY AND HOW DOES IT AFFECT US

Anxiety is defined as "an emotion characterized by feelings of tension, worried thoughts, and physical changes like increased blood pressure," (*Anxiety*, American Psychological Association, 2021).

Everyone experiences anxiety, some of us on a daily basis, but there is a vast difference between having normal feelings of anxiety or nervousness, and having an anxiety disorder in which our body cannot seem to snap out of its fight or flight response.

What is important to note is that anxiety and fear are not the same things. Fear focuses on an immediate threat and it is what we feel in the present, whereas anxiety is considered to be a future-oriented condition in which we try to diffuse a potential threat.

Fear, because it is present-based, is usually short-lived, whereas anxiety is long-acting, and is difficult to stop as we continuously try to ascertain what could go wrong next.

### Anxiety, Feelings, and Emotions

Most of us believe that our feelings and our emotions are one and the same thing, but they aren't, and for us to understand how anxiety and emotions are intertwined, we first need to differentiate between feelings and emotions.

Emotions are a physiological state that are generated subconsciously. They are a type of response that happens in our brain as a result of internal and external events. We have four basic emotions—anger, fear, happiness, and sadness.

Feelings are the subjective experiences we have as a result of our emotions. They are conscious decisions about how we react to our emotions. Our feelings include guilt, shame, confusion, rage, hopefulness, optimism, etc.

We cannot have feelings without first having emotions, but we can have emotions without feelings.

Anxiety is a response we have to our emotions, more specifically to the emotion of fear. While anxiety and fear are not the same things, they are interlinked, and this link is our feelings and thoughts.

When we feel stressed, our thoughts begin to run away from us and we feel anxiety, which creates a stress response. When we allow our thoughts and our inner critic to take over, our anxiety levels are increased and prolonged, essentially putting our body into a long-term stress response.

Added to this, anxiety releases adrenaline into our bodies, and when we have high levels of adrenaline in our bodies, it creates a stress response, which leads to trouble with emotional regulation.

It can be tough to distinguish between stress and anxiety and what role both of these play in our ability to regulate our feelings.

### Emotions Are Complicated

All emotions are complicated, and anxiety makes what we are feeling even more complicated.

Anxiety is caused by emotional fatigue because we are not processing what we feel or having the correct response to our fleeting emotions when they occur.

While emotions and anxiety are all related to our thoughts, stress, or circumstances, many times it is not the anxiety that is causing the feelings we are dealing with, but the incorrect processing of our emotions that is causing our anxiety.

Anxiety in itself can be stressful and can make us experience feelings that are difficult to manage. We may feel panicked, worried, sad, or overwhelmed as a result of our anxiety, and when we feel these things, our emotions are triggered.

Anxiety and emotions boil down to an inability to recognize or an unawareness of the connection between our emotions and our feelings. Poor coping skills also play a role, and it's these poor coping skills that have us turning to perfectionism.

When we are faced with a negative thought or feeling, we can become preoccupied with what comes next, and because our emotions are negative, we can sometimes feel that nothing good will come next. All of this triggers a fear response, and fear, as we know, is an emotion, driving our body into the right state to fight for its life.

### Anxiety and Anxiety Disorders: What Is the Difference?

Most of us will feel some form of anxiety at least once in our lives. We may describe it as excitement, butterflies in our stomachs, or nerves.

Anxiety is about as normal as breathing, but common anxiety and anxiety disorders are very different.

Having an anxiety disorder makes us feel a lot of pain and can get in the way of living a good life.

If we don't do anything about our anxiety, it will eventually have a big impact on our quality of life. As we try to fight off the exhausting feelings that come with anxiety, our relationships, ability to work, and drive to succeed can all suffer.

When anxiety happens too often, or when we experience fear that is out of proportion to what is happening, it is a problem and needs to be addressed so that we can build a life that we enjoy.

## WHAT CAUSES ANXIETY

Science isn't yet sure of the exact cause of anxiety disorders, but it does appear that anxiety can be triggered by something simple or a complex mix of things.

Some of the causes of anxiety disorders include

- a genetic predisposition to anxiety disorders.
- a difference in brain chemistry.
- environmental stresses including trauma or a stressful life.
- use or abuse of substances or withdrawal from these substances.
- medical conditions.

### *Symptoms of Anxiety*

Anxiety can manifest in different fears, but at the core of anxiety is excessive fear and worry.

When we have an anxiety disorder, we may find it difficult to eat, sleep, concentrate, and sometimes even breathe.

People experience different symptoms, though, and these can include some or all of the following:

- Panic attacks, feelings of ill ease, and fear.
- Feelings of impending danger or doom.
- Insomnia or trouble falling asleep or having interrupted sleep.
- An inability to remain focused.
- An inability to be calm or still.
- Having cold, clammy, or sweaty hands, or having a feeling of pins and needles in your extremities.

- Experiencing shortness of breath or breathing in a shallow way.
- Breathing too quickly or more often than is necessary.
- Heart palpitations
- Having a dry mouth, or feeling like there is a lump in your throat.
- Nausea and digestive discomfort.
- Tense, spasming, and painful muscles.
- Periods of dizziness or vertigo.
- Ruminating or intrusive thoughts.
- An inability to concentrate or remain focused on the issue at hand.
- A sudden, intense fear of things or places that weren't present before.

These are only some of the symptoms associated with anxiety, and having anxiety or a panic attack can sometimes feel so intense that we may feel gravely ill.

For some people, though, the opposite is true, and they may not recognize that they are dealing with anxiety until they have reached a stage of burnout.

We must become in tune with our bodies, learning to feel when something is not quite right so that we can rectify these issues before they threaten to overtake our lives.

## IS MY ANXIETY OUT OF CONTROL

Before you take the test below, I want to put your mind at ease. Anxiety is a very treatable condition, and you do not have to live a life filled with angst and the pain of anxious thoughts and feelings.

Look at the questions below, and answer them as honestly as you can.

| Question | Yes | Maybe | No |
|---|---|---|---|
| I worry about things a lot | | | |
| I have trouble controlling my worries | | | |
| When I am anxious I feel irritable | | | |
| My worries make me feel tired and worn out | | | |
| My worries keep me awake at night | | | |
| When I worry I find it hard to concentrate | | | |
| I feel jumpy and nervous a lot | | | |
| I worry about whether I am doing things well | | | |
| I worry about the future a lot | | | |
| I get headaches that have no medical explanation | | | |
| I find myself living in the past a lot | | | |
| My muscles ache when I worry | | | |
| When I worry, my thoughts become intrusive | | | |

If you have selected more yes and maybe answers than no answers, there is a good chance that you are battling with anxiety and will need to learn how to control how you are feeling.

## HOW ANXIETY AND PERFECTIONISM INTERTWINE

Perfectionism and anxiety can often go hand-in-hand, among other mental health issues that may develop as a result of our relentless pursuit of perfection.

A study conducted in 2016 explored the link between perfectionism and anxiety sensitivity and found that when we are concerned about making mistakes, or when we have personal standards that are too high, we are more likely to suffer from severe anxiety (Erozkan, 2016).

Added to this, anxiety can exacerbate our perfectionistic tendencies and *vice versa*. As perfectionists, we tend to judge our performance based on unrealistically high expectations, and we subconsciously know that we will not be able to achieve a perfect result, which causes us anxiety.

When we don't meet our unrealistic standards, we can exacerbate our anxiety, making us feel helpless and hopeless as we deplete our cognitive and emotional resources.

Anxiety and perfectionism can sometimes manifest as depression, eating disorders, OCD, and substance abuse disorders, and it can become really difficult to untangle the web of where anxiety and perfectionism meet.

## THE STEPS TO UNTANGLING PERFECTIONISM AND ANXIETY

When we're faced with negative thoughts, feelings, and emotions, it can be difficult to deal with. No one really wants to have to deal with negativity, but when we can acknowledge our emotions for what they are and make a conscious decision to act appropriately, it becomes easier to deal with negative situations.

Using the steps below, you can learn to better manage your negative emotions:

1. Observe your emotions by turning inward so that you can try and figure out what exactly is causing you to have these feelings.
2. Use one of the techniques in this book to help you manage your negative thoughts and inner critic.
3. Accept that it is okay to be vulnerable. When you don't validate your emotions and experiences they can manifest in negative behaviors.
4. Learn to challenge your thoughts and then distract your mind in a healthy way like deep breathing techniques and yoga.
5. Accept that having emotions is a part of life and that you are valid in your feelings.
6. Take a time out to think about why your inner critic has surfaced and how best to silence it.

7. Manage your stress by cutting out triggers in your life or changing your situation by learning to deal with stress correctly.

If anxiety is getting the better of you, use the following techniques to help you control your anxiety better:

1. Practice slow breathing so that you can distract your mind and regain control over your breathing function.
2. Stay present through mindfulness. When you can stay in the present rather than thinking about what is going to happen in the future you can halt the thoughts that create anxiety.
3. Take control of your health by eating well, getting active, and going out into nature. Not only will this reduce your stress, but it will show you how strong and capable you really are.
4. Use self-talk to your advantage by challenging negative thoughts and replacing them with positive scenarios in which you have overcome challenges and obstacles.
5. Set a time to worry and then do not allow yourself to worry again for the remainder of the day. Sometimes we just need to express all of the things we are feeling to be able to move forward.

6. Prioritize your sleep. If you aren't sleeping well everything will feel like a crisis you need to overcome.

## EXERCISES TO HELP YOU OVERCOME THE ANXIETY WHIRLWIND

Our normal rate of breathing is 10 to 12 breaths per minute. When we are anxious, our breathing rate either increases or decreases. This is called over-breathing and it can intensify the anxiety we are feeling, even tipping it into a full-blown panic attack.

### *Calming Technique*

Use this calming technique to help you reclaim your breathing and calm your mind.

1. Find a quiet place and sit or lie down in a comfortable position.
2. Close your eyes or focus on a specific spot.
3. Take a breath through your nose for a count of 4.
4. Hold this breath for a count of 2.
5. Now, release your breath for a count of 6 through your nose.
6. Pause for a count of 2 and begin again.
7. Repeat this process 10 times.

Calming techniques are designed to help you relax, but we can sometimes feel like we are getting them wrong. Practice over and over again until you are calm.

If you are going to stand up after your session, be sure to do so slowly to allow your body to readjust.

### Defeating Negative Self-Talk

Challenging our inner critics will help us to find all of the reasons we are amazing and unique, and will also assist in giving us the inner confidence to achieve our goals.

The exercise below is meant to help you question negative talk so you can easily change the way you think about it.

Make sure to read each of your column statements out loud so that they form a complete sentence so that you can reaffirm what you have written.

Reading out our thoughts is often more shocking than actually thinking them, and when we challenge them out loud, we can affirm that we are prepared to come to our defense.

I have completed the first three columns for you as an example.

| Thought | Distortion | Rational Response |
|---|---|---|
| My day really sucked! Everyone hates me because I was so unproductive! | <ul><li>All or nothing attitude</li><li>Exaggeration</li><li>Just not true!</li></ul> | Some days are better than others. People accept that I am human, and tomorrow will be a better day. |
|  |  |  |
|  |  |  |
|  |  |  |
|  |  |  |
|  |  |  |
|  |  |  |
|  |  |  |
|  |  |  |
|  |  |  |

Anxiety can feel like a freight train with no brakes sometimes, but you do have the power to manage your fear responses.

By using the information provided and learning to live in the present, anxiety can be reframed as positivity, hope, and happiness.

# 8

# TURNING PERFECTIONISM INTO A SUPERPOWER—THE SECRET TO INNER HAPPINESS AND PEACE

Perfectionism doesn't need to be defeated—it can become a superpower if you learn the art of inner peace and happiness and let go of the need to be perfect.

You don't need to climb a mountaintop to sit pretzeled in meditation, nor do you need to spend a year's earnings to attend a wellness retreat to find inner peace and happiness.

Simply making time for yourself to relax and get in touch with yourself is enough, especially in today's frantic-paced life.

We all need serenity and time to unwind, and by making this time for yourself, you can learn to draw on your inner peace when you need it the most.

Inner peace and happiness are states of spiritual and physical calm and are present despite the stressors we face in life. Having inner peace means finding contentment and happiness no matter how tough things get in our lives, and the best thing about inner peace and happiness is that you have control over it.

Perfectionism hinders our internal happiness because our inner critic, our attitude, and our fears control our thought processes. When we're aware of a potential problem, we fret, buckling under the stress of it.

But what if, instead of buckling, we rose from the ashes, hands on hips in a superhero pose, ready to take on the day?

Embracing imperfection, giving it everything we have every day, and finding the time to unwind and celebrate our day turns imperfection into the perfect weapon against negativity and internal conflict.

### The Secret to Being Happy

The secret to happiness is not as complicated as you may think, and it begins with a few simple steps to reclaim your inner peace.

### Step One: Focus on Positive Thinking

You have been provided with all the tools required to retrain your brain from negative to positive and to challenge your inner critic.

Recognizing the positive things in life is by no means downplaying the negatives that are happening. You are merely looking for the positives and not focusing on the negatives.

Never underestimate the power of recognizing all of the silver linings life shows you.

## Step Two: Celebrate the Victories

It doesn't matter how small or big they are, victories are meant to be celebrated. Life is always going to be full of ups and downs, and when you take the time to recognize and celebrate the small wins.

Taking pleasure in the little achievements shows you exactly how much you do accomplish in a day and will open your eyes to how important small steps are in achieving a lofty goal.

## Step Three: Accept That You Are Perfectly Imperfect

Just about everything in life that is great is imperfect, and we only ever get to experience these things when we accept the opportunity to embrace their imperfection.

Strictly speaking, engineers know how to make sure planes stay in the sky, but scientifically speaking, the metal giants shouldn't be able to take off, let alone remain in the sky for miles on end. Yet somehow, most of us will, at some point in our lives, buckle in and take to the skies, trusting the imperfectly perfect design of a plane.

You are no different from others in your imperfect design—trust that you can fly!

## Step Four: Do The Things You Love

It's a pretty tough ask to be happy if you're only doing things that you hate. You cannot waste your life on things that do not spark joy in you. Find your passion and your purpose so that you can get up every day looking forward to life.

## Step Five: Build Positive Relationships

We all know at least one person who seems to have nothing good to say about anything. Don't allow yourself to be sucked into anyone else's negative spiral.

You deserve to be happy, and you deserve to have relationships that are positive, encouraging, and uplifting.

## Step Six: Let It Go!

In the words of a Disney princess, let it go!

You cannot hold onto your worries forever. Worry may give you something to do, but it is counterproductive and will only ever waste your time.

Set aside a small amount of time every day to allow yourself to worry and then let it go and get on with the business of being happy.

Finding inner peace is far easier when we can learn the art of positive thinking. Combining inner peace and realistically optimistic thoughts will have your well-being at an all-time high.

### How to Become a Positive Thinker

Positive thinking is a great stress management tool and can help you remain firmly grounded in the present, which assists in keeping anxiety at bay.

Added to this, realistic optimism is one of the best ways to silence negative self-talk, and can even help you improve your overall health.

### Make Use of Positive Mantras

While it is true that happiness can come from external things, it also comes from internal joy, peace, and happiness.

This is especially true if your inner critic is particularly persistent, and to combat these negative thoughts, it is a good idea to counter them with positive mantras that will boost your confidence.

### Focus on Your Successes

It's easy to see how amazing we are when we focus on the positive things we have done and accomplished.

For you to start thinking more positively, you will need to remind yourself regularly that you have been successful in the past and you will be successful in the future.

**Find Role Models**

Finding positive role models who reflect your values and purpose will help you to see the benefits of being positive.

Added to this, when we have positive role models, we can draw inspiration from their journey, showing us that we can all overcome obstacles and hardship with the right mindset.

**Stay in the Present**

Planning for the future is great, but you need to do things in the present so that you can achieve your goal in the future.

Learn to live in the present and when you find yourself dwelling on the past or future, choose to acknowledge your thoughts and then come back to the present moment.

**Surround Yourself With Positivity**

Spend time doing the things that make you feel happy and positive. This can be listening to music, reading, watching positive films, or spending time with people who love you or uplift you.

Positive influences affect your state of mind, and it's nearly impossible to feel down in the dumps when you're surrounded by the things that make you happy.

## Focus on Solutions

Pessimists will focus on the problems they are facing, while optimists will problem-solve so that they can focus on solutions.

It's human nature to want to focus on the problems we are facing, but focusing on what solutions are available to you will help you see that there is light at the end of the tunnel.

Life isn't fair sometimes, but when we can accept that it is not our circumstances but what we do with our circumstances that counts, we change our mindset and begin to see the proactive plans that will change our circumstances.

Finally, always remember that tomorrow is another day, and as long as you are continuing to work on your happiness and your well-being, you are well on your way to learning how to become a positive thinker.

### *Steps to Turning Perfectionism Into a Superpower*

Believe it or not, perfectionist tendencies are not all bad if you choose the right behaviors. It takes a whole lot of strength to strive toward something unattainable, and if we look at it logically, you are already setting lofty goals for yourself.

It is not perfectionism that is holding you back; it is your mindset, and when you change your mindset, you can turn being a perfectionist into a superpower.

**Step One: Know the Pros and Cons**

Like everything else in the world, there are pros and cons to being a perfectionist. If you feel like you are sliding into perfectionism, take a look at these pros and cons and choose to focus on the pros.

**Step Two: Set Your Goals Not Someone Else's**

Any goals you set are for yourself and not for anyone else. Setting personal goals makes them easier to attain and allows you to draw on resources you already have within yourself.

**Step Three: Be Mindful of Sliding Into Perfectionism**

Make sure that you are setting tasks for yourself to do with a specific time limit so that you can get things done rather than get stuck in planning and procrastinating. If you are not able to complete your tasks in a realistic time frame, chances are that you are sliding into perfectionist tendencies.

**Step Four: Allow Yourself to Make Mistakes**

Remember, mistakes are not fatal and they're certainly not bad. Celebrate your mistakes, learn from them, and then move on.

**Step Five: Take it Easy On Yourself**

As a perfectionist, you place the most pressure on yourself. Remember to practice self-compassion and kindness by lowering your expectations. There is no such thing as perfection, so learn to be proud of doing your best.

## Step Six: Learn to Take Criticism

Build your self-esteem so that you can learn to accept criticism as an amazing opportunity to grow and develop. Criticism, especially when it is constructive, is healthy and provides you with the feedback you need to help you achieve your goals.

## Step Seven: Cut Out Negativity

You will need to be mindful of how much negativity you are subjecting your subconscious mind to. Social media, the news, and television can reinforce negativity and perfectionism.

Remember that what we see on the internet and on social media is designed to promote a narrative that is not your own.

## POSITIVE MANTRA TO FUEL YOUR SUPERPOWERS

Mantras help us to heal and to reinforce our capabilities.

The words we use daily, both out loud and inside our minds, have a profound effect on how well we cope emotionally and mentally.

Try to use your mantra in a way that resonates with you. If you believe you're more inclined to hear the mantra by using your first name, then change the mantras below so that they fit with what works best for you.

### Superpower Mantras

1. I am strong
2. I am myself
3. I am enough
4. I have everything I need inside of me
5. I deserve success
6. I am resilient
7. Fear does not rule me
8. I am a warrior, not a worrier
9. I am at peace
10. I only work for my higher good
11. I am exactly where I need to be
12. Negative thoughts only have power over me if I allow them
13. I do not judge myself or others
14. I am worthy
15. I am perfectly imperfect

A constant quest for perfectionism can slow down our productivity enormously, but perfectionism is an element of being a high achiever if you know how to harness your inner power.

Above all else, being a perfectionist strips you of your joy and your happiness in life. It leads you to believe you are incapable when, in fact, you are capable of taking charge of as many great things as you ever set out to do.

# CONCLUSION

So many of us believe that we are strong because we are perfectionists. We fail to realize that our perfectionism is crippling us until it is too late, and we are stuck in a spiral of analysis paralysis that causes us anxiety, depression, and extreme frustration at our lack of productivity.

Even though we know we are to blame, but we can't get over our annoying need to be perfect.

The irony is not lost on that sentiment either, as we know that no one is to blame for our tardiness, or procrastination other than ourselves, and no matter how hard we try to free ourselves from the constraints of perfectionism, our inner critic comes knocking at the door of our conscious mind, telling us anything less than perfection is an invitation for failure.

But failure is needed to succeed, so is vulnerability, and a deep need to want to change our perfectionist ways.

For many of us, we were the A+ student—the child who was described as detail-oriented, favoring quality over quantity of work. We were the loners, preferring to hold ourselves to the ridiculously high standards we set for ourselves rather than deal with the diligent student who put out a quantity of work yet somehow managed to achieve more than we did.

We become so entrenched in the idea that the habits of perfectionism are what make us great, that external validation and approval are the only things that drive us, and we become fearful, berating ourselves when we believe that our efforts are just not enough.

The first time we experience failure, we believe that our world has ended and that our failure in completing a task perfectly, or at all, means that we are a failure.

The reality is that most of what we accomplish in life, from taking our first steps to driving a car, and even our first perfect project, all started with failure and with an internal drive that told us to try again.

We have to learn to step outside of our comfort zones, trying things we aren't good at, no matter how anxious it makes us because growth is needed for us, to become high achievers.

To cultivate the right mindset for overcoming our fears and moving forward in life, we must turn inward, becoming vulnerable with ourselves and others. We need to embrace the fear we are feeling and then just take a leap into the unknown so that we can discover what it is about ourselves that truly sets us apart from the next person.

Ditching being perfect will be the best thing you ever do for yourself, and it will be the most empowering transformation you will ever make.

In reading this book, you have a route mapped out for you. Choose to stop, reprogram your GPS, and drive yourself to success. Choose to enjoy your own personal journey to success, and always remember—you have only ever failed if you are no longer prepared to try.

Get up!

Dust off!

Try, try, and try again!

# REFERENCES

American Psychological Association. (2021). *Anxiety.* Apa.org. https://www.apa.org/topics/anxiety

Appel, H., Englich, B., & Burghardt, J. (2021). "I Know What I Like" – Indecisiveness Is Unrelated to Behavioral Indicators of Evaluation Difficulties. *Frontiers in Psychology, 12.* https://doi.org/10.3389/fpsyg.2021.710880

*BrainyQuote-I have not failed, I've just found 10,000 ways that won't work.* (2019). BrainyQuote. https://www.brainyquote.com/quotes/thomas_a_edison_132683

Clear, J. (2014, March 6). *How Long Does it Take to Form a Habit? Backed by Science.* James Clear. https://jamesclear.com/new-habit

Cole, N. (2015, October 22). *The Mindset of High Achievers.* Observer. https://www.google.com/url?q=https://observer.com/2015/10/the-mindset-of-high-achievers/

*Definition of failure.* (2019). Merriam-Webster. https://www.merriam-webster.com/dictionary/failure

*Definition of mindset.* (n.d.). Merriam-Webster. https://www.merriam-webster.com/dictionary/mindset

*Definition of perfectionism.* (n.d.). Dictionary. https://www.dictionary.com/browse/perfectionism

Dweck, C. (2015). *Carol Dweck Revisits the "Growth Mindset."* Student achievement. https://studentachievement.org/wp-content/uploads/Carol-Dweck-Revisits-the-Growth-Mindset.pdf

Erozkan, A. (2016). Understanding the Role of Dimensions of Perfectionism on Anxiety Sensitivity. *Universal Journal of Educational Research, 4(7),* 1652–1659. https://doi.org/10.13189/ujer.2016.040717

Gautreau, C. M., Sherry, S. B., Mushquash, A. R., & Stewart, S. H. (2015). Is self-critical perfectionism an antecedent of or a consequence of social anxiety, or both? A 12-month, three-wave longitudinal study. *Personality and Individual Differences, 82,* 125–130. https://doi.org/10.1016/j.paid.2015.03.005

Giffin, E. (2004). *Something borrowed-I am learning that perfection isn't what matters. In fact, it's the very thing that can destroy you if you let it.* St. Martins Press.

Grover, S., Mattoo, S., Gupta, N., & Painuly, N. (2011). Anger attacks in obsessive compulsive disorder. *Industrial Psychiatry Journal, 20*(2), 115. https://doi.org/10.4103/0972-6748.102501

Intern. (2022, April 14). *Perfectionism in the Workplace.* Momentum. https://momentumleaders.org/2022/04/14/perfectionism-in-the-workplace/

Isaacson, W. (2021). *Steve Job.* Simon & Schuster.

Jung, C. (2019). *A quote by C.G. Jung.* Goodreads. https://www.goodreads.com/quotes/44379-until-you-make-the-unconscious-conscious-it-will-direct-your

Konyenikan, I. (n.d.). *A quote from Wealth for All-Failure is constructive feedback that tells you to try a different approach to accomplish what you want.* Goodreads. Retrieved September 21, 2022, from https://www.goodreads.com/quotes/7172739-failure-is-constructive-feedback-that-tells-you-to-try-a

*Meditation for Guidance: Strengthen the Inner Voice.* (n.d.). 3HO International. Retrieved September 18, 2022, from https://www.3ho.org/meditation/meditation-for-guidance-strengthen-the-inner-voice/

*Merriam-Webster Dictionary.* (2022). Merriam-Webster. https://www.merriam-webster.com/dictionary/inner%20speech

*Perfectionism Test.* (2019). Psychology Today. https://www.psychologytoday.com/us/tests/personality/perfectionism-test

Primack, B. A., Shensa, A., Sidani, J. E., Whaite, E. O., Lin, L. yi, Rosen, D., Colditz, J. B., Radovic, A., & Miller, E. (2017). *Social Media Use and Perceived Social Isolation Among Young Adults in the U.S. American Journal of Preventive Medicine, 53*(1), 1–8. https://doi.org/10.1016/j.amepre.2017.01.010

Puchalska-Wasyl, M. M. (2014). Self-Talk: Conversation With Oneself? On the Types of Internal Interlocutors. *The Journal of Psychology, 149*(5), 443–460. https://doi.org/10.1080/00223980.2014.896772

*Quote from Pearls Of Eternity—Success in life is not for those who run fast, but for those who keep running and always on the move.* (n.d.). Goodreads. Retrieved September 12, 2022, from https://www.goodreads.com/quotes/7890685-success-in-life-is-not-for-those-who-run-fast

van Gaal, S., de Lange, F. P., & Cohen, M. X. (2012). The role of consciousness in cognitive control and decision making. *Frontiers in Human Neuroscience*, 6. https://doi.org/10.3389/fnhum.2012.00121

Yaribeygi, H., Panahi, Y., Sahraei, H., Johnston, T. P., & Sahebkar, A. (2017). The impact of stress on body function: *A review*. *EXCLI Journal*, 16(1), 1057–1072. https://doi.org/10.17179/excli2017-480

Made in the USA
Monee, IL
07 May 2023